100 Content Marketing Tips

Learn How to Drive Thousands of Visitors to Your Blog

By Tamas Torok

Contents

Important Disclaimer

The author has made every effort to ensure the accuracy of the information within this book was correct at time of publication. The author does not assume and hereby disclaims any liability to any party for any loss, damage, or disruption caused by errors or omissions, whether such errors or omissions result from accident, negligence, or any other cause.

Bonus Resources

You can get instant access to 5 additional tips, downloadable worksheets, checklists, a list of resources and links mentioned in this book.

I highly recommend you unlock this bonus package to get the most out of this book.

CONTENTMARKETINGTIP.COM/RESOURCES

20 Years Ago...

I used to spend a lot of time with my father when I was 7 years old. Back then, he had a small grocery shop close to our home town. I spent most of my afternoons hanging around, talking and playing with the employees. I discovered secret places and played hide and seek mostly with myself.

But after a few weeks it wasn't that exciting anymore. Employees got busy, along with my father, and I had discovered everything in the shop. So now I had to figure how to kill time.

My father got tired of me telling him that 'I'm bored', so he decided it was the perfect time to teach me how to create paper airplanes. He took a minute break and showed me how to assemble a basic model.

Not surprisingly, my first versions barely could fly, rather they just fell down. But I started practicing and my models eventually got better. They could even fly a few meters without falling down. I was so proud.

After learning the minimum skills, it wasn't that challenging to create a basic model anymore. I became the expert of basic paper planes in the grocery shop. But I got bored again.

So I started brainstorming ideas on how to make my airplanes look cooler, fly faster and longer. I experimented with small tricks like bending the rear of the plane to make it more stable (honestly, I didn't care about physics), I also tweaked the wings to make them look cooler, I even colored some of them to scare the enemy. None of my tricks were scientifically proven, they were just my imagination.

I tried so many things to improve my paper planes and some of them didn't work at all. You can imagine what happened when I bent back the front of the plane. But hey, some experiments worked pretty well and this is what really mattered.

It took me almost 15 years to realize that those experiments gave the highest boost to my airplane construction success. I could say that I developed my own agile method to continuously improve my paper planes through these small experiments.

I want you to do the same in content marketing.

Experiment with the curiosity of a 7-year old child. Think outside of the box, brainstorm, let your imagination flow and try even the craziest ideas. These regular experiments are what really move the needle in the long term.

Who Is This Book for?

This book is for bloggers, content marketers and any other unmentioned professionals who are determined to boost growth with the power of content marketing.

It doesn't matter if you just started building your content marketing strategy from scratch or you already have one. There are always new things to discover and room for further improvement.

What's in it for me?

There is a lot of talk going on about content marketing in today's fast paced society. Not only is more content created every year, but there are a lot of people publishing great content on many different aspects of the topic. It's quite overwhelming and feels like there are so many things you can try to improve your content marketing strategy.

There's a lot of value packed into this book, but these tips aren't here to overwhelm you. They are here to inspire and guide you to successfully take your content marketing to the next level.

I'm giving you actionable tips with step-by-step instructions on how to implement them, tools you can use and additional reading if you want to learn more. They cover the most crucial aspects of content marketing.

These tactics are used by the most successful bloggers and content marketers to grow their business. With this book, you will do the same by:

- Creating a strong foundation for your blog
- Learning about your niche and competitors
- Discovering new ways to get in touch with your audience
- Getting relevant organic traffic
- Receiving more engagement and traffic from social media
- Generating more leads and subscribers
- Improving conversion rates
- Keeping more people coming back to your website

How to use this book

I recommend two strategies for reading this book:

1. **Scanner method**: Go through this book from front to back. Discover the tips, get inspired and come up with your own

experiments. As you read the tips, make notes and mark the most interesting ones you would like to go to back later.

2. **Sniper method**: If you already know the area where your content marketing needs the most improvement, you can simply jump to that chapter and focus on those tactics.

This book is your handbook during your adventure. Read it, put it down, experiment, come back and read again.

Part 1: The Process: Shifting to an Experimental Mindset

Alright, you know that you should switch to an experimental mindset when you start working on implementing these tips.

But executing *all* of these tips at once just to save some time and give your blog an instant boost will lead to exactly the opposite. You will get extremely busy doing everything without achieving much. Trust me, I did exactly this.

I have been talking about tips and tricks a lot, but what we need first is a process. You need a defined process, because what worked for others may not work for you. Since your audience is different, your content is different and your business model might be different, as well.

There is no one magic tactic that will skyrocket your blog's growth, but rather these tactics add up and will lead to continuous growth. It's like continuously improving your paper plane by experimenting with different folding techniques.

This process allows you to constantly learn from your audience by running focused experiments and eventually take your content marketing to the next level and drive growth to your service or product.

Set Measurable Goals

All you need to do is to set clear goals with time frames and key results you would like to achieve.

- **Objective**: What is the one thing you can achieve that will drive the biggest impact on your blog?

- **Time Frame:** When do you want to achieve it?

- **Key Results**: Quantitative measurements that indicate if you're achieving an objective.

During this process, I recommend this free Excel template; just <u>click here to download it</u> among with some bonus stuff. Here are the steps you should follow:

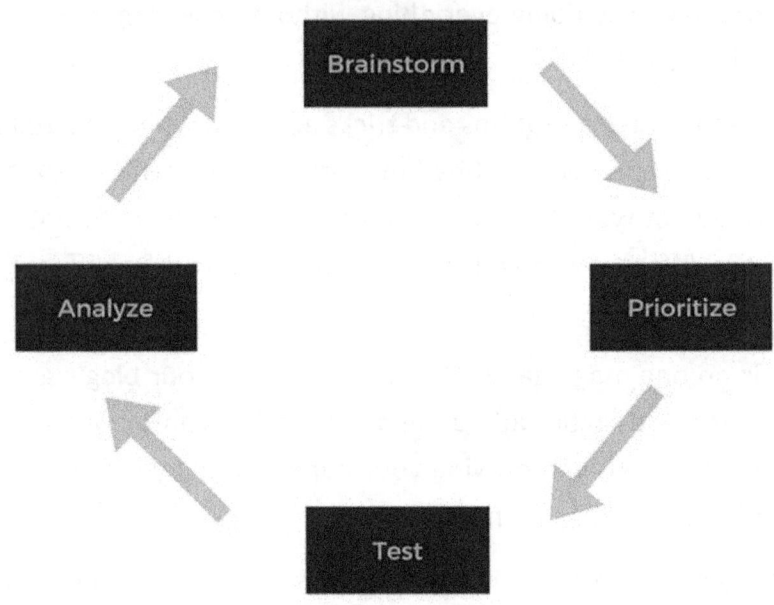

1. **Brainstorm**: Check out the 100 tips and even come up with your own ideas. Brainstorm on the inputs, not on the outputs, which means that you should determine the elements that directly affect the area you want to improve. Let's say you want to improve email open rates, what are the elements that influence that? What tactics can you try? Put your ideas into the backlog section of the Excel template.

2. **Prioritize**: We're looking for the low-hanging fruits that are easy to implement but the potential positive impact is relatively high. Consider the probability of success, potential impact and resources needed to execute that tip. Create a prioritized list in the Excel template under the experiments sheet.

3. **Test**: How can you test your hypothesis? How can you get enough data to validate or invalidate your hypothesis? A test is valid if the objective, time frame and key results are clearly defined.

4. **Analyze**: Success or failure? What was its impact? Why did you see those results?

Analyze your results in the Excel sheet. What did you learn? What are the key takeaways from that experiment?

Part 2: Create content people want to read

I'm sure you don't want to spend time creating content no one wants to read. This chapter will help you figure out what content to write and gives you some tips on how to make them remarkable and shareable.

1. Learn more about your audience

Learning more about your target audience isn't what directly affects your content promotion efforts, but if you don't spend time on it, then the foundation of your content marketing is going to be very weak and you won't see significant improvement, even after implementing all the content promotion tips here. First, you need to create buyer personas to see what their lives look like.

Buyer personas are semi-fictional, generalized representations of your ideal customers. They help you understand your potential customers better, making it easier to tailor your content to their real needs.

It's not just valuable when you start out, but also when you have an established blog. You have to regularly revise your buyer personas to make sure you're on the right track.

Step 1: I'm sure you already have some assumptions regarding your target audience's needs and problems. You also have some tips on who they are and what demographic they fall into. Assumptions are great to get started, but not enough to build your content marketing on. Fill out this buyer persona template with your assumptions.

Step 2: Get out of the building. You need to talk with these people in order to validate and invalidate your assumptions. But instead of asking just random questions, you need to ask the right questions. Here are some rules you should keep in mind:

- You shouldn't ask anyone whether your business is a good idea.
- Don't tell your customers what their problem is during the interview.
- Keep customer interview meetings casual, as a friendly conversation.

To identify their problems, I like to use the following questions:

- What are your biggest challenges in <your field>? (Identifying pain points)
- What have you done to overcome these issues? (Level of determination)
- How do you find the necessary info you need? (Where and how are they looking for information)
- What content format do you enjoy the most? (How do they prefer to learn)

Use the '5 whys' technique to dig deeper and find the root cause of the problem. With this technique you need to transform yourself into a 3-year old kid who just keeps asking why all the time. Here is an example:

1. **Why?** - The battery is dead.
2. **Why?** - The alternator is not functioning.
3. **Why?** - The alternator belt has broken.
4. **Why?** - The alternator belt was well beyond its useful service life and not replaced.

5. **Why?** - The vehicle was not maintained according to the recommended service schedule. (root cause)

But how many people should you talk with? You don't have to aim for statistical significance. Our goal is to see important patterns in their answers. According to a user research expert, Jakob Nielsen, <u>85 percent of the problems are observed</u> after doing just five interviews in the same audience segment.

Step 3: Based on the answers you received, go back to your buyer persona template and update it. Now you are seeing a real picture of your target audience so you can start focusing on creating content that actually provides value to them.

Tools:

<u>Mturk</u>

<u>Craigslist</u>

Recommended reading:

<u>Create Buyer Personas for Your Business [Temlate]</u>

<u>20 Questions to Ask When Creating Buyer Personas [Free Template]</u>

<u>Summary of 'The Mom Test'</u>

<u>The Complete, Actionable Guide to Marketing Personas</u>

2. Always stay on the right track

It's super easy to get lost in the nitty-gritty details of content marketing. New social networks emerge, new tactics pop-up and Facebook and Google algorithms change all the time.

Sometimes we just get into the loop and don't really realize what and why we are doing what we're doing. I did it quite often.

Buzzstream put together a list of questions that gives a bird's eye view on your content marketing strategy and helps you identify its weak points.

I recommend you use it not only when you start building a blog from scratch, but also when you already have one and need to do a regular content marketing audit:

1. *Who is your audience?*

    Beginner golf players.

2. *What are you offering them?*

    Tips and tutorials on how to improve their skills.

3. *How will they find you?*

    Through search engines and influential sport sites.

4. *Why will they care?*

    Easy to try tips to help them improve dramatically.

5. *How will they interact?*

    They will watch videos and read blog posts.

6. *What will be their next step?*

    Signing up for your private training webinar.

7. *Why do they share it?*

Presents them in positive light, they want to impress peers.

8. *They might not share it if...*

Their peers might think golf is just for wealthy people.

9. *A solution for this...*

Proving that golf is available for everyone.

Recommended reading:

Get Heard, Get Seen, and Get Traffic with Standout Content Promotion

Why You Need to Conduct a Full Audit for Successful Content Marketing

The Step-by-Step Guide to Conducting a Content Audit

3. Find your audience through your competitors

It's a huge challenge finding new channels to reach your target audience. If you run out of ideas, you could try a different approach: your competitors.

Analyzing your competitor's website could reveal some really interesting information, including audience and main traffic sources. If you find a traffic source that generates traffic to your competitor's website, then that's probably a viable channel for you, too. You can even copy their user acquisition techniques.

Step 1: Create a list of your closest competitors. If you don't know them or just want to update your list, try one of the following methods:

- Search Google by using your top keywords

- Use this query to find similar websites (related: competitorwebsite.com)

- Enter your competitor's domain on SimilarWeb.com

- Submit their Facebook page's link to Likealyzer (see the similar brands section)

Step 2: Enter competitor's domain on SimilarWeb.com to see where their visitors are coming from, which social networks they use and see what's interesting for that audience.

Tip: If you want to learn more about your competitors, check out tip 4 on competitor analysis.

Tools:

SimilarWeb

Likealyzer

Recommended reading:

How to Find Your Target Audience

How To Find Your Target Audience And Create The Best Content That Connects

20 Best Competitor Research Tools

4. Easily spy on your competitors

How do your competitors drive traffic to their website? What are they doing on social media? Do their posts actually get engagement or not? By following the steps below, you can get a detailed picture of your competitor's traffic sources and social media activity.

Step 1: Go to Similarweb.com and submit your competitor's URL. This is where the magic happens.

This report gives you more information about your competitor's website:

- Total visits (incl. Avg. visit duration, pages per visit and bounce rate)
- Traffic by countries
- Traffic sources (Direct, referrals, search, social, mail, display)
- Detailed insights on referral traffic
- Search traffic (with organic and paid keywords)
- Social traffic structure
- Audience interest
- Other websites people visit
- List of similar websites

Step 2: To learn more about your competitor's social media activity, use Fanpage karma and Buzzsumo to reveal more information, such as:

- What is their avg. engagement rate?
- How often do they post?
- When are they posting?

- What type of posts are they posting?

- Best performing content (by using Buzzsumo)

For a more detailed fan page analysis, try Likealyzer. It gives you metrics on likes, growth and engagement.

To analyze anyone's Twitter profile, check out Twitonomy. It will show some general information, such as average tweets per day, total retweets and favorites. Twitonomy will also break down how many of your competitor's tweets contained links, hashtags, mentions and also received replies and retweets. All you need to do is enter the handle on the left side, under the "Analyze a Twitter profile" section.

Step 3: To learn more about their SEO performance, SE Ranking gives brief information on the top 10 websites for each of your queries: keywords ranking organically, in PPC campaigns, traffic channels and key SEO metrics including backlink profiles.

As a free alternative, I like to use OpenLinkProfiler for doing some backlink research.

Tools:

SimilarWeb

Twitonomy

OpenLinkProfiler

Likealyzer

SE Ranking

Fanpage Karma

Recommended reading:

15 Awesome Tools for SEO Competitor Analysis

10 Competitive Analysis Tools: How to Analyze Competitors Websites

How to Find Your Competitors Online and Knock Them Out

5. Purple cow and your content

One of my favorite books is Seth Godin's *Purple Cow,* which starts with a great story...

You're driving your car on a road surrounded by green meadows with cows hanging around. You probably won't remember any of their color patterns and won't talk to anyone about the cows, because they're almost all the same and there is nothing special about a bunch of cows anyway.

But what if you spot a purple cow among the many brown ones? A purple cow is remarkable, a purple cow is something you will remember, a purple cow is something you will talk about.

When you create content, you release your own cow to the meadow. How do you make sure that it's remarkable?

I'm sure we can agree that creating remarkable content is hard. The bad news is that it's becoming even harder to stand out. More than 2 million blog posts are published every single day and 77% of B2C marketers said that they'll increase their content marketing efforts. Meaning they will push out even more content. The meadow is just getting more crowded with cows.

It will be even more challenging to cut through the noise with your content.

Simply creating more content is not enough. The era of '500-word me too fluffy' content is over. Creating high quality content is still not enough, but much better than focusing solely on quantity.

What you need to do is to create high-quality content that stands out from the crowd, that delivers value in a unique way and that shows a radically new perspective. You need to create purple cow content.

19

I know, it's really hard. It's easier said than done. With this tip I would like to show you a framework that can be used to create your own purple cow content. There is no guarantee that all of your content will be a huge success, but if you follow a structured way then your chances of creating remarkable content will dramatically increase. Feel free to tailor this framework to your own preferences.

1. Format: what kind of content formats are published in your niche? Would your audience prefer a different type, such as an infographic or video?

2. Headline: do your headlines trigger emotions and make people want to check out your content? For some headline tips, check out tip 6 below this section.

3. Content: should you be more specific, more actionable? Do you offer something no one else can in your niche? Presenting your own findings and case studies are quite effective.

4. Story: do you tell stories that keep your audience reading your content?

5. Length: should you create longer or shorter articles for your audience? Do you know what they really prefer?

6. Visuals: is there a unique visual way to present data or explain your points?

7. Topic: what niches are you focusing on? What topics have not been covered? Can you add something to the already covered ones?

8. Giveaways: do you offer something additional for your readers they can download or access?

9. Context: where and how is your content presented? What does your blog look like?

10. Secret sauce: What makes people talk about your content? Check out tip 7 on how to create content that goes viral.

Recommended reading:

Create Content That Is Truly Unique: How to Find Your Tilt

2 Million Blog Posts Are Written Every Day, Here's How You Can Stand Out

Purple Cow, New Edition: Transform Your Business by Being Remarkable--Includes new bonus chapter

6. Secrets of catchy headlines

Just imagine a situation where you have a great article with a boring headline that doesn't trigger emotions or create a curiosity gap. I can already hear the crickets chirping...

You need to build content promotion into your content. This is the foundation of every successful content promotion campaign, and it starts with writing an irresistible headline.

Did you know that on average, 8 out of 10 people will read a headline, but only 2 out of 10 will check out your post? This is the first step when people decide to leave it or click it.

But you also have to avoid creating clickbait headlines. A typical clickbait headline relies on sensationalism, creates a huge curiosity gap and over promises the value readers will receive after clicking, but not delivering on that promise.

It takes time and practice to create a catchy title. When you craft a headline for your next post, just follow these steps:

Step 0: You have to make sure that the topic, content type, and format resonates with your audience. Your headline has to be catchy, but also relevant. See tip 59 below on how to research keywords for your blog post.

Step 1: Write at least 10 headline variations that meet at least one or two of the following requirements: urgent, unique, useful, ultra-specific. Read more about these here.

Step 2: It's time to test your headlines. Paste them to CoSchedule's headline analyzer or an emotional headline analyzer to get a detailed analysis. A score above 70 is good enough.

Step 3: Now you have everything you need to decide which headline variations are the most promising. If the results are not satisfying, start the process again. If you run out of ideas, you can try a headline generator (see tools) as a refresher.

Step 4: What does your audience say? Choose the best (3-4) headlines and promote your content on social media with these different variations. After a few hours, you will see the engagement of each headline, so keep the best performing ones.

Pro tip: In Google search, a headline with a relatively high click-through rate will receive a ranking boost since it indicates that the post is more relevant for that search query.

Note: Don't over promise in the title. Even though it may make people click, as soon as they realize you tricked them, they will leave your website, which is a sign of bad quality for Google. Posts with clickbait headlines are also penalized on Facebook. Don't sacrifice short-term gains over long-term ones.

Tools:

CoSchedule's Headline Analyzer

Emotional Marketing Value Headline Analyzer

Headline Generator

Recommended reading:

How to Write Viral Headlines: New BuzzSumo Research

52 Headline Hacks

19 Headline Writing Tips for More Clickable, Shareable Blog Posts

4 U's: Copywriting Tips for Great Headlines & Copy

7. Build promotion into your content

The success of your content promotion efforts highly depends on the content you have created. If your content is not good enough, then you can't expect significant results after trying the following promotion tips. There is a reason why so many people say that content is king. It simply determines the foundation of your content promotion efforts. Without great content you can't get too far.

I'm a big fan of Jonah Berger's book, *Contagious*. In his book, Jonah did extensive research on why some things go viral and others don't. The result of his research is a framework containing seven principles that determine the success of every idea, product and service. These principles can be applied to your content as well.

When you create your content, I recommend you follow this framework. It simply helps you create something that people want to share and talk about. It seems easy to do so, but it's actually much harder to execute.

Here is a framework you should follow when you create your content:

- **Social currency**: people like to seem smart and cool in front of others. Try to create content that makes people feel this way. Make them feel they're 'insiders'.

- **Triggers**: how can you make sure that people are frequently reminded about your content? 'Top of mind' also means 'tip on tongue'.

- **Emotion**: emotional content often goes viral so make sure it triggers high arousal emotions.

- **Public**: the more public something is, the more likely people will imitate. It's especially true for design products.

- **Practical Value**: content that is valuable and useful gets shared. Create something people can use right away.

- **Stories**: people like stories because they stick and are easy to pass on. Create stories people want to tell.

Your content doesn't have to meet all of these principles, but the more you meet, the better your chances will be to create something people want to talk about.

Recommended reading:

Contagious resources

Contagious: Why Things Catch On

Made to Stick: Why Some Ideas Survive and Others Die

8. Keep readers longer on your content

You're playing in the attention game. Believe it or not, your readers have a very limited attention span.

A Microsoft study demonstrated that the average human attention span while online is 8 seconds. What's really interesting to me is that it was 12 seconds in the year 2000. This study has a very important message for you: you have just 8 seconds to grab your reader's attention. Tough thing!

When they open your content, the countdown starts from 8 seconds. How do you convince them to stay and read your stuff?

Fortunately, there is a proven introduction template that actually hooks readers. It's called the APP method:

- **Agree**: start with a concept your reader will agree with. Example: "Nowadays it's really hard to stand out with your content"

- **Promise**: in the promise part, you show the reader a better world, creating contrast between the current and an ideal state. Example: "It turns out, you can easily create content that stands out from the crowd and people will remember"

- **Preview**: show them what they get when they read your content. Example: "In this post, I'm going to show you a formula that helps you easily differentiate your content"

To keep your visitors reading your content, use Bucket brigade. It was used for sales letters to keep prospects reading the full offer. This tactic can be applied to your content as well. Here are some example phrases you could insert in your content to keep your readers reading:

- Here's the deal:

- Now:

- What's the bottom line?

- You might be wondering:

- This is crazy:

- It gets better/worse:

- But here's the kicker:

- Want to know the best part?

You also have to structure your text, make your content digestible by using sections and use simple sentences to make it easier to read and understand.

Tools:

Hemingway App

Readability Checker

Readability Grader

Recommended reading:

Awesome! 16 Powerful SEO Copywriting Secrets (That Work Fast)

How to Make Visitors Read Your Entire Article

How to Get Blog Visitors to Read Your Entire Post

9. Get free, high-quality images

Images play a crucial part in content marketing. It catches your audience's attention and makes your content easier to consume and understand. I'm sure you know that you can't skip including images in your blog post. Adding images isn't a big deal, but finding high-quality images is the true challenge. You can find plenty of images on Google, but most of them are lame or protected by copyright.

If you still use generic stock photos in your content (the ones with people smiling in an unimaginable situation) then please stop, I have much better alternatives:

- Life of Pix
- Splitshire
- Little Visuals
- Stocksnap
- Unsplash
- Gratisography
- Picjumbo
- Publicdomain Archive
- Death to the Stock Photo
- Move East
- *See 19 more in the bonus resources*

Part 3: Build your Network

Content marketing is about building meaningful relationships. In this chapter, you will find some tips on efficiently building relationships with customers, partners and industry influencers.

10. How to build relationships with other humans

I know it sounds weird, a tip on building relationship with others. You may think that this book is supposed to be about content marketing tips, not about social advice. But trust me, it's super important.

The problem is not with our ability to build relationships with others but rather that we often forget to use our social skills online.

Building meaningful relationships with fellow bloggers, target audience and influencers is the foundation of every successful outreach campaign.

Honestly, it's quite tempting to skip this part and I made a huge mistake when I did that. I simply didn't care about building meaningful connections with the people in my outreach campaigns. I went for the quick, short-term wins instead of building relationships with people. I just sent out emails and expected people to become frantic fans of me. I failed.

But honestly, why would they do that?

- They don't know me

- I just appeared out of the blue

- They're not as interested in my stuff as I think

- I asked a favor

- They're busy

I don't know what I did expect, really...I still regret this mistake and I don't want you to fall into the same trap. So in this tip, I collected 12 different ways to start building relationships with others. I'm sure you can use most of them to be more successful in long-term relationship building. This list goes from the easiest ways to the hardest, more complex ones.

1. Follow them on social media (Twitter, Facebook, Instagram) where ever it is applicable. On Twitter, you can add them to a list; make sure that list is public so they will receive a notification when they are added.

2. Engage their content (like, comment) on social media

3. Share their stuff on social media

4. Subscribe to their newsletter

5. Leave meaningful comments on their blog posts

6. Give them feedback

7. Ask them how you could help their latest project/campaign

8. Do interviews with them

9. Ask their advice on something related to your field

10. Buy their book, attend their webinars, support their crowdfunding campaign (works well with influencers), make sure you let them know via email

11. Meet up somewhere: conference, for a coffee

12. Don't rely on creepy, prewritten templates. As the famous quote says: be yourself, everyone else is already taken.

Tools:

Nimble

Contentmarketer.io

Recommended reading:

How to Win Friends and Influence People

11. How to find anyone's email address

Getting in touch with fellow marketers, influencers and your target audience is a significant part of content marketing. We build relationships by creating content and when it comes to promotion, we reach out to influencers, friends and people who might benefit from our content. Social media and other communities are great to keep in touch with your network, but email is still the most effective way to do that.

But you know, email addresses aren't that easy to find. So I thought I would try to help you by sharing 5 ways to find anyone's email address.

Method 1: Check the target person's website. You will probably find a "Contact" or an "About" tab where their email address may be mentioned. Did you find it? Great job!

Method 2: Search for the person on LinkedIn. If you can find their profile, just scroll down and see if they set the preferred method of contact. In some cases, you can find an email address there. Bingo.

Method 3: If you're familiar with the structure of the company's email address then you can simply guess your target person's email address or use this tool to generate different variations. Copy these suggestions and put them into an email validator tool to see which one is valid.

Method 4: Install Sidekick's or Rapportive chrome extension. Log in to your Gmail account and compose a new message. In the "to" section insert the different email variations you generated for a person. If the information appears in their contact profile section then the email address is valid.

Tamas Torok

torok.tomi@gmail.com

London, United Kingdom

Edit your profile if it's not up-to-date.

Inbound Marketer | Growth Hacker | Blogger | Full-stack Marketer | Author |

Author at 100 Content Marketing Tips

LinkedIn

support | privacy   rapportive

Method 5: Whols can help you uncover the email address that was originally used to register the domain. All you need to do is paste the URL of the person's website and search for the email with which it was registered. This method works best with personal websites.

Tools:

Emailhunter

Mailtester

Validate Email Address

Whols

Rapportive

Voila Norbert

Find Any Email

12. Build a tribe

I recently finished reading a book from Jeff Walker in his book, called *Launch,* he describes how to plan and execute successful product launches. Among many valuable takeaways, there is one thing that everyone should keep in mind: build your following early.

These are people who're interested in your stuff, who can't wait to find a solution for their pains or needs. In your content marketing, you should follow exactly the same method; you need to build a tribe.

It's not only important when you start out, but also when you already have an established follower base. These people can validate your ideas; they provide feedback and help you by sharing your stuff with their friends.

It takes time to find these people, get in touch and keep the relationship active. But if you can collect 50-100 people for your blog then you will be on the right path.

Step 1: You need to figure out where you can find these people. It's important to get people who are in your target audience. Where do they hang out? Do they attend festivals or conferences? Are there any niche social networks or groups for them? Here are some tips to get started:

- Facebook and Google groups

- LinkedIn

- Niche social networks

- Forums

- Festivals, conferences and other offline events

Step 2: Create a list of these people in an Excel sheet or you can add them to a CRM such as Nimble. Research their email address (see tip 11 for more details) and social media profiles.

Step 3: Get in touch with them one-by-one. In every single case, find a unique reason to start a conversation. This reason could be: an article both of you liked, an event you attended, a group you're both members of, etc. Most of them will reply to your emails.

Step 4: Now you're not an absolute stranger to them, since you already have something in common. Once you come up with an idea or a new post related to their interest, you have a tribe to go to and get some feedback on your work.

Note: don't always just ask for their feedback. That's just a one-way relationship. Try to give something back. Follow them on social media, share their stuff, and mention them in your article or social media. Always let them know that you're there if they need anything. It truly makes the difference. Read tip 10 to learn about building meaningful relationships online.

Tools:

Nimble

Contentmarketer.io

Recommended reading:

The Complete Guide to Building Your Personal Brand

How To Find Your Target Audience And Create The Best Content That Connects

How to Use Twitter to Build Relationships for Your Business

Launch: An Internet Millionaire's Secret Formula To Sell Almost Anything Online

13. Build relationships with influencers

Getting influencers to share your content is a really satisfying moment; it feels like winning the lottery. Indeed, it's a really powerful way to amplify your content reach, but often people think that a list of influencers and a well-written pitch is enough for success.

Unfortunately, 99% of the time this approach does not deliver results. I'm sure you heard that you have to build relationships with them and the sad truth is that it doesn't happen overnight. It takes weeks and even months. I used to be that creepy guy who created a long list of people and busted them with lots of 'not so well' written emails. Fortunately, I tried a more patient, slower approach that actually worked. In this tip I'm sharing it with you.

Step 1: Find relevant influencers who can easily reach your target audience. Simply search for "top influencers" or "influencers" with your keyword such as "content marketing" and see if somebody has already created a list. If not, you can use Buzzsumo to create your own list.

Step 2: In Buzzsumo, select the influencer tab and search for a keyword related to your niche. You will get a long list of relevant people. Set up your filters according to your preferences and focus on the most relevant people.

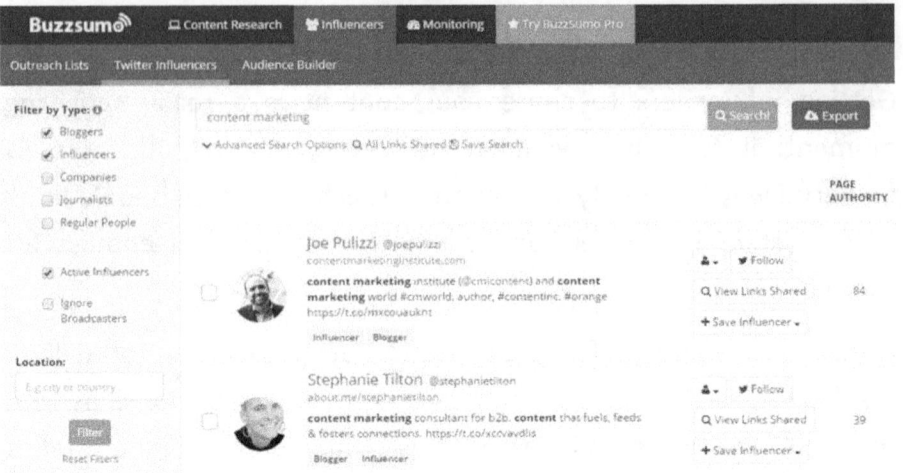

Step 3: There are many ways to build relationships with them so you need to figure out what works best in your niche (check out tip 10 for some actionable tactics). Our goal is to build tremendous value in their life. Do these tactics consistently for at least 5-6 weeks.

Step 4: Keep your email short and sweet, make sure that you add your own personality and don't rely heavily on templates. I suggest you do not ask for a share directly. Ask for feedback on your content; let them say what they think about your stuff. If they think it's awesome, then two things can happen: 1. They automatically share it or 2. Don't share it. In this case, you could politely ask them if they could help you spread the love.

Pro tip: Don't approach your influencers every time you publish something. It's really annoying in the long run and you can easily burn down your relationship. I would recommend that you approach them every other month when you have a truly amazing thing to share.

Note: influencer outreach in itself is a huge topic that could be a new book. With this tip, I wanted to give you a framework to follow. For greater details, please check out the recommended resources below.

Tools:

Buzzsumo

Contentmarketer.io

Nimble

Recommended reading:

Blogger Outreach: How to Get Influencers to Promote Your Content for Free

How I Got An 80% Response Rate For My Top Influencers Outreach Campaign

How To Find Influencers To Amplify Your Content Marketing

5 Strategies to Get Top Influencers to Share Your Content

Part 4: Social Media Tips

This section will reveal a huge amount of actionable social media marketing tips. You will learn how to get followers on the main social media platforms, increase engagement and also how to drive more traffic to your blog.

14. Get 1000 Twitter followers within a week

Twitter is quite an open social network so it's pretty easy to get in touch with others. In this tip, I show you how you can capitalize on this openness and get 1000 new targeted followers within one week.

Step 1: There are two different methods you can follow:

Stealing competitor's followers:

Create a list of Twitter accounts your target audience probably follows. The best way to start with is your competitors. I recommend using Crowdfire or Statusbrew for that.

Keyword-based targeting:

Let's take "blogger" as an example. If you use this keyword, then you will see everyone who mentions "blogger" in their profile. For keyword-based follower copying, use Narrow.

Step 2: Download Crowdfire, Statusbrew (smartphone apps) or sign up for Narrow (web app) and set up your account. These are tools that help you manage followers and non-followers. The use-case for each application is pretty similar. In the following steps, I'm using Crowdfire to show you exactly how to copy other's followers.

Step 3: Under the copy followers menu, add the Twitter accounts selected at Step 1.

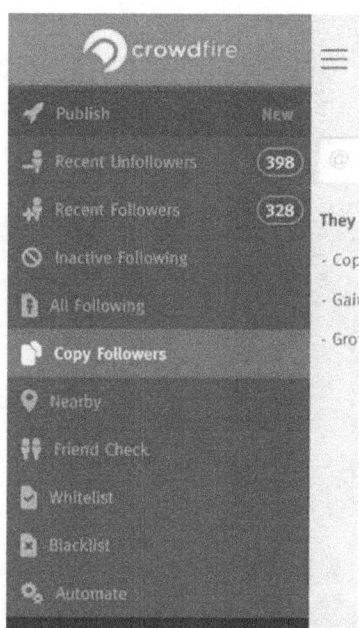

Step 4: The app will list the followers of the selected Twitter accounts. Start following these people. But be careful; don't just blindly follow everyone on that list since you can easily add a lot of creepy, not so cool people as well. This is how I accidentally (really!) started following a porn star. Keep in mind that quality is more important than quantity.

Step 5: You should expect to see that 20-30% of the followed people will follow you back. After a day, unfollow everyone who didn't follow you back by using the mentioned applications (unfollow feature).

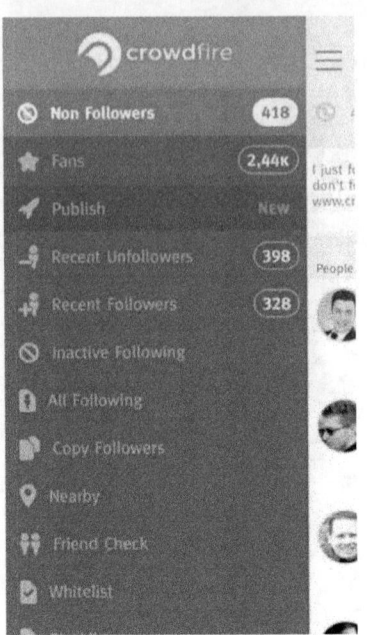

Tools:

Crowdfire

Narrow

Statusbrew

Recommended reading:

How to Get More Followers on Twitter Fast

7 Ways I Accidentally Got More Twitter Followers (and 7 Ways You Can on Purpose!)

How to get More Twitter Followers (The Ultimate Twitter Tips Guide)

How to Attract and Engage More Twitter Followers

15. Get more engagement with embedded tweets

You can embed already shared updates from Twitter to your blog post. It takes just one click for your readers to engage with your post. An embedded tweet not only stands out from your blog post, but it is also a sign of social proof. It can increase engagement, further extending your reach on Twitter.

Step 1: Login to your Twitter account and go to your updates.

Step 2: Select the tweet you would like to embed.

Step 3: Click on the 3 dots at the bottom of your tweet.

Step 4: From the list, select "Embed Tweet."

Step 5: Copy the code and insert it into your blog post.

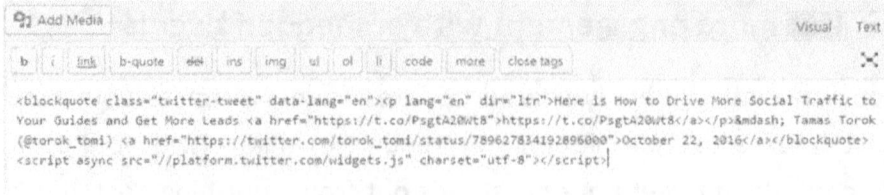

```
<blockquote class="twitter-tweet" data-lang="en"><p lang="en" dir="ltr">Here is How to Drive More Social Traffic to
Your Guides and Get More Leads <a href="https://t.co/PsgtA20Wt8">https://t.co/PsgtA20Wt8</a></p>&mdash; Tamas Torok
(@torok_tomi) <a href="https://twitter.com/torok_tomi/status/789627834192896000">October 22, 2016</a></blockquote>
<script async src="//platform.twitter.com/widgets.js" charset="utf-8"></script>
```

This is how it should look:

Pro tip: If you want to align your embedded tweet to center, modify this part of the code (<blockquote class="twitter-tweet" data-lang="en">) to this (<blockquote class="twitter-tweet **tw-align-center**" data-lang="en">).

Recommended reading:

Tips, Tricks & Best Practices to Increase Twitter Engagement

19 Best Examples of How Top Brands Use Twitter

20 Tips for Increasing Twitter Engagement

16. Reach out to people who shared similar content

Reaching out to random people and asking them to share your stuff isn't really a promising and efficient tactic. We need to find people who already expressed interest toward a specific topic. These people, when approached with relevant content, will probably read it, give feedback or even share it with their followers.

This is what we are looking for. You have to find people who have already shared similar content and ask them to check out your content as well.

Step 1: Create a list of articles with links that are similar or closely related to your content.

Step 2: On Buzzsumo.com, paste these links one-by-one. Submit the link and click on "View Sharers". It will show you everyone who shared that content. It's a paid feature, but you can try it for free and see how this tip actually works for you.

Step 3: Add these people to a list and start approaching them on Twitter. Make sure you don't send out the same tweet to too many people in a short period of time (that's spamming). Instead, create different variations, keep it short, take your time and you will be fine.

Tools:

Buzzsumo

Recommended reading:

15 Experts on how they develop an outreach strategy

5 Tips For Using Twitter To Pitch Your Story

17. The power of pinned tweets

Do you have a blog post that you would like to highlight on your Twitter feed to get more engagement and some traffic boost?

With pinned tweets, you can easily stick one of your tweets to the top of your profile page, making it really easy to notice for everyone who visits your profile page. This is a great way to get some extra engagement and traffic to your blog post.

Check out some Twitter profiles and see the engagement rate of pinned tweets. Now compare them to other, not pinned ones. You will see a remarkable difference between engagement rates.

Step 1: Visit your profile on Twitter and select the tweet you would like to feature on the top of your profile. You can pin only your own tweets.

Step 2: On the bottom of your tweet, click the three dots and select "Pin to your profile page" from the dropdown menu.

After refreshing the page, your tweet should be pinned to the top:

Recommended reading:

You Will Get More Retweets If You Do This ONE Simple Thing

How To Get The Most Out Of Pinned Tweets

How To Write The Perfect Tweet

18. Optimize your Twitter schedule

It does matter when you share updates on Twitter. Some people suggest focusing on the time when the activity of your followers is the highest. Others say that you should share your stuff when your audience's activity is lower to avoid competition and easier to get their attention.

No matter if you share the busiest or less busy time, our ultimate goal is to get the biggest attention possible for our updates. You need to know when your audience is the most and least active so you can start experimenting with different posting schedules.

Step 1: Go to Tweriod.com and sign up for a free account with your Twitter account. Tweriod will show you the most and least active periods of your followers.

Step 2: Once you're in, click on the "My analysis" menu and it will show you the time range when you will get the most exposure. You can also see when your customers are the most active during weekdays and weekends (according to your Twitter account's time zone).

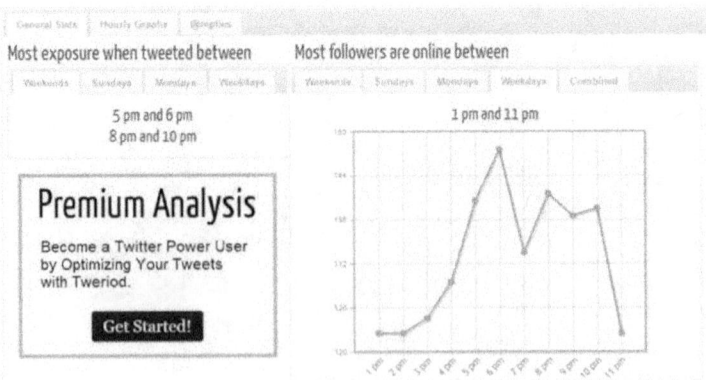

Step 3: In Buffer, create a new schedule based on your audience's activity. From the menu, click "Schedule" and set up different post times for weekdays and weekends.

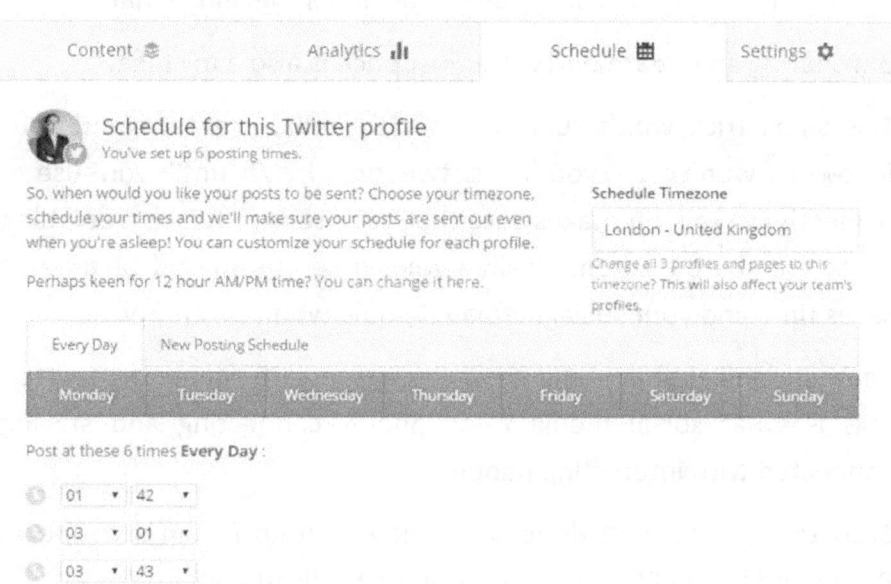

Every time you add a new post to your Buffer, it will share it according to this schedule.

Tools:

Tweriod

Buffer

Recommended reading:

The Biggest Social Media Science Study: What 4.8 Million Tweets Say About the Best Time to Tweet

The Best Time to Post on Facebook, Twitter, and Instagram in 2016

Infographic of the week: Best times to post on social media

19. Put your Twitter promotion on autopilot

It's not as creepy as it sounds. Fully automating your Twitter account is the worst thing you can do on social media. Never do that.

But sharing an update on Twitter just once is also a mistake.

This small trick won't ruin your social media presence and your followers won't see you as a tweeting R2D2 until you use it respectfully. This tip makes sure that your selected, evergreen blog posts are shared automatically within a certain period of time. It saves time and your social media schedule won't be empty.

Keep in mind that you still have to engage with others on Twitter. This is what social media is all about, connecting and staying connected with interesting people.

Step 1: If you haven't done so already, sign up for an account on Buffer and for IFTTT (connects different applications).

Step 2: In Buffer, set up your own update schedule by selecting "Schedule" from the upper menu. Make sure the time zone matches the settings of your Twitter account.

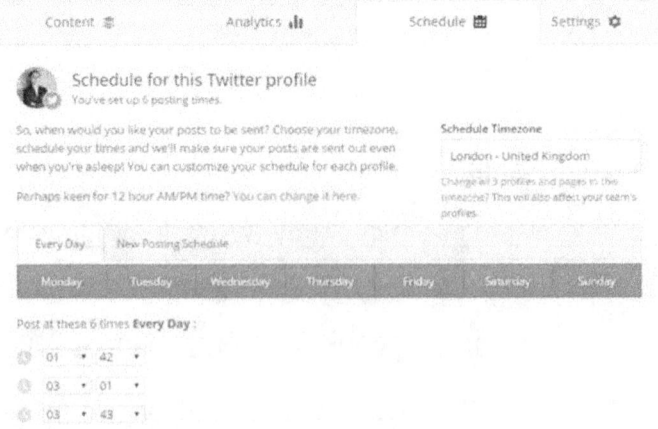

Step 3: In IFTTT, add this recipe and follow the instructions during the setup process. You need to connect your Buffer and Twitter accounts to make it work. Once you're finished, your tweets will be automatically rescheduled in Buffer.

Tools:

Buffer

IFTTT

Recipe I'm using

Recommended reading:

Infographic: How Often Should You Post on Social Media? See the Most Popular Research and Tips

What are the Best Times to Post on #Facebook, #Twitter and #Instagram? [INFOGRAPHIC]

What 16 Studies Say About The Best Times To Post On Social Media

20. Boost social shares with your fans

I'm sure you have noticed that there are some people who quite often engage with your posts on Twitter. A handful of people who are your fans, who relentlessly like and retweet your stuff.

You shouldn't just let those people be there without getting in touch. They could be a great source of feedback and also, with their help, you can amplify your content as well. If you have an engaged follower base, then you can use this tip with great efficiency.

Since Twitter is a bit noisy, sometimes it's worth giving your most engaged fans a quick heads up when you have something new to share. Here is how you can capitalize on your fans on Twitter.

Step 1: In your Twitter account, go to your notifications page to see all the interactions your followers and others did in the past with your tweets.

Cole Hromek and 7 others followed you   6h

Fabrizio Bianchi liked your Tweet   19h
19h: Scrum for Marketing: How We Get 50% More Things Done
without Working More #Scrum

Laurie Jamaitus liked your Tweet   Oct 20
Oct 20: 50+ Content Promotion Tips That Will Skyrocket Your
Content 🖐 #ContentPromotion #Traffic

Ana O Hidalgo liked your Tweet   Oct 20
Oct 20: 50+ Content Promotion Tips That Will Skyrocket Your
Content 🖐 #ContentPromotion #Traffic

Listing Depot, **logodesignser** and **TwExList** followed you   Oct 20

Step 2: Create a list of these people who shared, liked or retweeted your previous updates. You can use a spreadsheet or Nimble for that, which is a CRM system that helps you keep in touch with your network.

Step 3: Get in touch and thank them for engaging with your posts. You can follow them back and also share their stuff. I like to add these people to a separate Twitter list. When you start following someone, click on the gear next to the follow icon and from the list, select "Add or remove from lists". Then simply create a new list or add them to an existing list.

Step 4: Once you have a new post to share, get in touch with these people (via Twitter or email) and ask for their feedback or just kindly suggest your post to read. If they like it, they will share it. If you prefer to send them an email, check out tip 11 to find out their email addresses.

Tools:

Nimble

Recommended reading:

5 Tips for Interacting with People You Admire on Twitter

The Ultimate Guide to Targeting Twitter Users and Connecting With Influencers

The #1 Mistake We All Make on Twitter (It's Probably Not What You're Expecting)

21. Reach out to your target audience

It's pretty easy to get in touch with everyone on Twitter. In this tip, I'm showing you how you can find people from your target audience and get some extra shares for your content.

We're not begging for shares, we're building relationships with your audience by involving them in our content creation process.

Step 1: Do you know what keywords describe your target audience the best? Think about what words they might use in their updates and profile description.

Step 2: Go to your Twitter account and search for these keywords. Make sure that you put your keywords in quotation marks so you will get exact matches for those keywords. You can also use Buzzsumo to list these people and filter them according to their follower base and influence.

Step 3: Follow and add them to a list on Twitter.

Step 4: When you have the first, unpublished version of your content, reach out to these people and ask their feedback on your content. In this case, you are involving them in the content creation process so once you publish it, they will be more likely to share it. You can get some extra exposure, but also get valuable feedback on your content, making sure that it will meet your audience's expectations.

Tools:

Buzzsumo

Recommended reading:

How to Use Twitter Lists to Follow Thousands (and Appear Superhuman)

22. Mention sources in your social media posts

You can expect to receive extra engagement by mentioning others in your Twitter updates. When you share a new post on Twitter, make sure to include one or two handles of your sources so when you post, they will be notified and hopefully like or retweet your update. Create different tweet variations and mention a maximum of two different sources in every single tweet.

Step 1: Search for the Twitter handles of your resources.

Step 2: Create different headline variations for your tweets and add 1-2 different handles to each. Make sure to craft catchy headlines, see tip 6.

Step 3: Share your tweet at different times (leave a few hours between each tweet) and see how the mentioned people engage with them. Buffer is a great tool to schedule updates in advance.

Tools:

Buffer

Recommended reading:

The #1 Mistake We All Make on Twitter (It's Probably Not What You're Expecting)

Twitter Mentions 101: Tracking and Finding

Twitter Mention

23. Retweet boost for your tweets

You can easily give a retweet boost to your freshly published content. Just Retweet is a platform where members earn credits for retweeting other people's tweets.

I know, it might sound bad. Buying retweets is like buying random followers on Twitter. But even if the person who retweets your tweet doesn't belong to your target audience, you can still reach your audience through them.

A few initial retweets for your posts could give it momentum so you can reach a broader audience. Fortunately, in Just Retweet, you can set up requirements, such as interest, and a minimum number of followers, so only people who meet them will be able to see it and retweet it.

Step 1: Register at Justretweet.com by signing in with your Twitter account. You will automatically receive some points so you can use them to submit your own tweets.

Step 2: Click "Submit tweet" and craft your tweet and fill out the necessary fields. Select the appropriate category and set the minimum number of Twitter followers an account needs to be able to retweet your tweet.

Step 3: Submit your tweet and retweets should start coming soon. Make sure to measure the engagement your retweeted post gets and also check if it actually drives traffic to your blog or not.

Tip: If you would like to collect more points without actually paying for it, search for tweets related to your field and if they meet your quality standards, feel free to retweet them.

Tools:

Just Retweet

Recommended reading:

The 10 Most Clickable Twitter Headlines

15 Twitter Headline Templates That Pull Twitter Traffic

How to Write an Engaging Twitter Headline

24. Reverse giveaways

There are many successful blogs out there with incredibly popular and well converting giveaways. Appsumo used viral giveaways to grow their subscriber base from zero to 500 thousand. Bloggers like Neil Patel and Brian Dean generate thousands of subscribers from their free, downloadable content. The good news is that you can capitalize on their success.

With this tip, you will get access to anyone's audience who shared a specific giveaway. You can expect this highly engaged and relevant group to share and download your content as well.

Step 1: Create a list of successful giveaways in your niche. It's worth having a look at your competitors' and other related sites where your target audience hangs out. Save their titles and links in a spreadsheet.

Step 2: Pick the link of the most promising giveaway and enter it to Buzzsumo to see how many people shared it on Twitter.

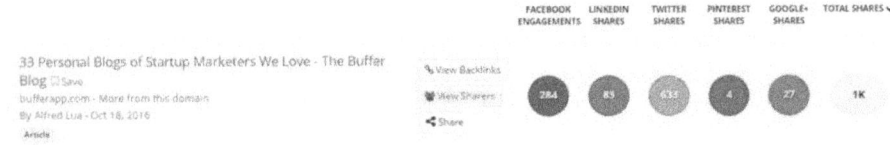

Step 3: Create a list of people who shared it on Twitter. They are highly interested in that topic so chances are they will check out your content as well.

Step 4: Create a giveaway that is related to your field and the popular giveaway.

Step 5: Let them know via Twitter that you have content that might be interesting for them. Write a short pitch like: I saw that you shared <popular giveaway> so I thought you may also like <Your giveaway>.

If you prefer sending emails, check out tip 11 on how to find their email addresses.

Tools:

Buzzsumo

Recommended reading:

Reaching out without creeping out: Your 101 guide to building your network online

10 Ways to Approach a Stranger via Twitter

21 Content Promotion Strategies That Will Triple Your Traffic

25. Higher engagement with GIFs

One tweet (and generally other social media updates) only reaches a fraction of our follower base. But even if some of your followers see it, that doesn't mean they will engage with your update. Their social media wall is really crowded; hundreds of posts are competing for their attention.

Your tweet's lifespan is just one hour. If you can't get engagement within the first hour then probably you won't get any after that. If you want to get retweets, replies and clickthroughs, you have to make your tweet stand out from the crowd. Apart from optimizing your tweeting schedule, using hashtags and paying attention to tweet length, you can use GIFs to make your tweet stand out and boost its engagement.

- When you're sharing an update on Twitter, attach a GIF by clicking on the "GIF" button on the bottom of your tweet.

- Try to attach a GIF that matches your update. If you can't find an appropriate one, then try Giphy

- If you have time, you can create your own GIF by using this free tool.

Tools:

Gifmaker

Giphy

Recommended reading:

The Life of a Tweet: A Look at the First 24 Hours

How to Find the Perfect GIF: 10 Must-Try Websites

10 Awesome Websites to Find The Best Animated Gifs

26. Highlight and share

Did you notice that when some people (or even you) read an article online they tend to click and highlight some words or sentences? People typically do it when they read something interesting. It also keeps them focused on the content and makes it easier to navigate within the article.

SumoMe has a tool that helps you capitalize on this habit. Once your reader highlights a piece of text from your article, the Highlighter app will generate a tweet and recommend to share it on social media. This makes it much easier for your readers to share a quote, a sentence or just a few catchy words.

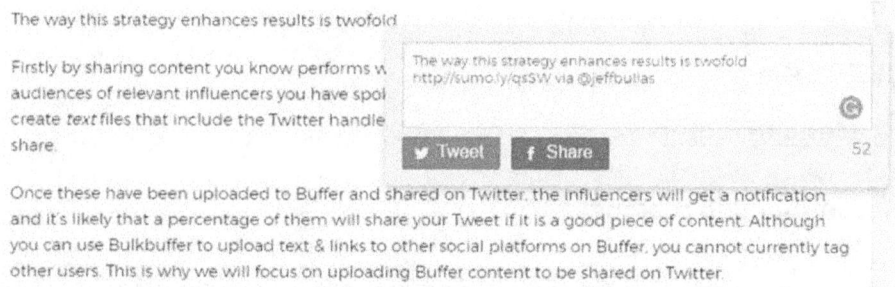

Step 1: Register at sumome.com. You should copy and paste SumoMe's code to the <head> section of your website. If your blog is running on Wordpress, then there is a free plugin that helps you easily edit your website's header and footer.

Step 2: On your website's left or right side you should see a small blue tab with the SumoMe icon. Here is how it should look:

From the tool menu, select the Highlighter app and add it to your website.

Pro tip: Once you set up SumoMe's highlighter tool, don't just leave it running. Make sure you measure the results it delivers. Does it actually generate more social shares?

Tools:

SumoMe

Header and footer plugin

Recommended reading:

How I Used SumoMe to Increase My Email List By 10x Overnight

15 Free Alternatives to SumoMe's Software Suite

27. Optimize your Tweets

Millions of tweets are published every day and chances are that your followers also receive lots of updates. Their news feed is pretty crowded so it's a big challenge to grab their attention and convince them to click and check out your content.

I collected some tips that can help you make your tweets more visible, achieve higher engagement and get higher clickthrough rates.

Keep in mind that these tips and best practices aren't here to blindly follow, but rather to inspire you to run your own experiments.

Shorter tweets are easier to read and better for retweeting (your tweet won't be cut off). Try to keep it around 120 characters.

Always include images in your tweet. Tweets with images are 94% more likely to get retweeted, and 89% more likely to get favorited.

Sometimes ask for a retweet. Salesforce found that tweets that specifically ask followers to "Retweet" receive 12 times higher retweet rates.

Use one or two relevant hashtags to get two times more engagement. Use Ritetag for finding the perfect hashtag for your tweet.

Perfect timing. You can achieve 30% higher engagement if you post during the day (between 8AM-7PM).

According to KISSMetrics, retweets are the highest around 5 pm and the best time to post for higher clickthrough rate is 6pm. Use Tweriod to get to know when your followers are the most active.

If you're sharing a stat, article or a quote from another Twitter user, make sure to include her handle in your tweet. This will increase the likelihood of retweets and favorites from that person.

Insert your link as close to the beginning of your tweet as possible. Links placed earlier in a tweet receive much higher clickthrough rates than links placed at the end of a tweet.

Shorten your links to improve the appearance of your tweet and get additional tracking information.

Tools:

Tweriod

Ritetag

Recommended reading:

A Scientific Guide to Writing Great Tweets: How To Get More Clicks, Retweets and Reach

The Science of Social Timing

28. Optimize your Facebook posts

A news feed algorithm takes into account many different ranking factors related to post type and what a certain post contains. When it comes to crafting your post, you should pay attention to the following elements:

- Post Type
- Post Text
- Headline
- Image

Your selected post type depends on the preference of your audience. Run experiments and figure out which resonates with them the best. Here are some best practices you should follow:

- Avoid using clickbait headlines (it will hurt your news feed rank). Check out tip 6 for some headline tips.

- Use hashtags (60% increases in interactions).

- Posts with questions get 23% more engagement.

- Keep link title less than 100 characters.

- Tag related pages, when it makes sense.

- Engage fans with photos (93% of the most engaged posts contain photos). If you share a link, let Facebook pull the image of your articles.

- Remove links from link copy after Facebook pulled in the image and title.

- Use emoticons.

Recommended reading:

[Anatomy of a Perfect Facebook Post: Exactly What to Post to Get Better Results](#)

[7 Tips for Crafting the Perfect Facebook Post](#)

[How to Craft the Perfect Facebook Post](#)

29. Hidden opportunities in Facebook groups

Facebook provides great opportunities to connect with people interested in many different fields. Really, you can find countless groups from dog breeding to healthy living. These groups are small niche communities within Facebook and they provide excellent opportunities to:

- Get to know your target audience

- Promote your content

Step 1: Create a list of keywords that best describe your niche.

Step 2: Perform some searches on Facebook. Enter your keywords in the search field and hit search. From the upper menu, click on the "Groups" tab.

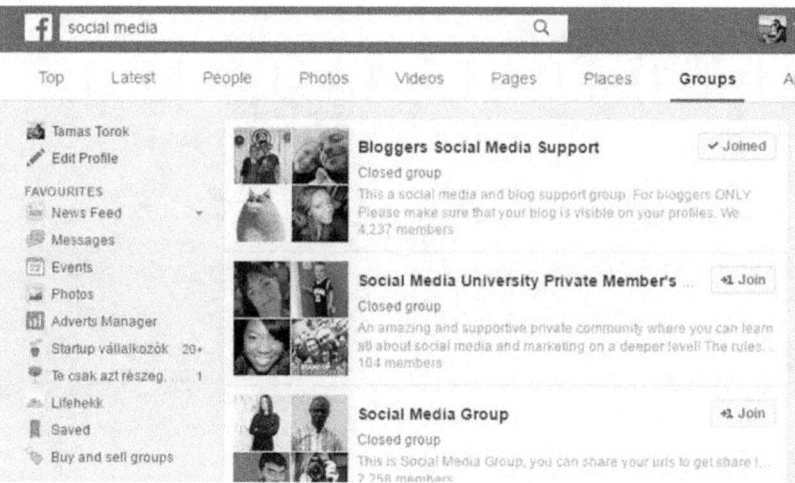

Step 3: After joining groups, do not share your content right away. Read the rules first and take part in the conversations. Bring value to the community by answering questions and helping others.

Step 4: The most appropriate way to share your content is when someone asks a related question and your content helps them solve that issue. Another way is to share it like an update and ask for feedback from the group members.

Recommended reading:

6 Clever Ways to Use Facebook Groups for Marketing Your Business

6 Clever Ways to Use Facebook Groups for Growing Your Business

Facebook Groups Marketing: 5 Success Tips

30. Convert blog visitors to Facebook fans

Growing your Facebook fan base is pretty damn hard. Obviously you can kickstart growing your follower base by inviting some friends to like your page, but this is what everybody does and in most cases after a short 'like' rush, nothing really happens. You have fans, but not really your target audience. So you need a different approach; what if you try to get fans from your website?

This is a great way to grow your Facebook following and you will probably get more relevant fans, since they already expressed their interest by visiting your website. If they really liked your stuff, they will want to keep in touch with you.

Step 1: We're setting up an exit intent pop-up for getting more likes. This pop-up will show up when your reader intends to leave your blog. There is a free tool called Hellobar you can use to test this tip.

Step 2: After registration, create a new exit intent pop-up with the goal to get Facebook likes. Make sure to add the URL of your Facebook page. Customize the text, design and we're all set. Here is how the final result should look:

Follow Neil Patel on Facebook
Get free marketing and business advice!

Tools:

Hellobar

Recommended reading:

Wait..Don't Go!: 4 Ways to Use Exit-Intent Popups Effectively
7 Best Practices for Using Exit-intent Popovers, Popups
7 Little Known Ways To Get More Out of Your Conversions from Your
Exit-Intent Popups

31. More engagement with embedded Facebook posts

By embedding a Facebook post to your blog post, you can make it much easier for your readers to like or share your post. If you want to get more engagement on Facebook, then you definitely need to try this tip.

Step 1: Login to your Facebook page and select the post you would like to embed. Make sure the post image appears and looks great.

Step 2: Select the small arrow from the top right corner of the post.

Step 3: From the menu, choose "Embed."

Step 4: Copy the code and insert it into your blog post.

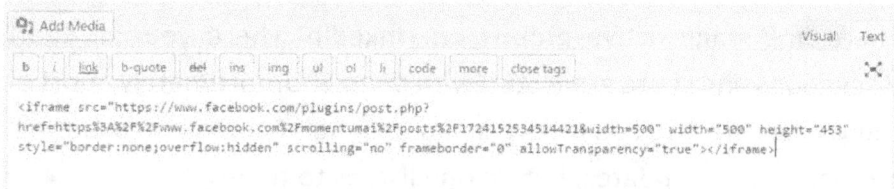

Here is how it should look:

Recommended reading:

8 Sure-Fire Facebook Post Formulas That Drive Engagement

How to Increase Your Facebook Engagement by 275%

How to Improve Facebook Engagement: Insights From 1bn Posts

32. Share your content in LinkedIn Groups

There are many active groups on LinkedIn where you can start discussions and share great stuff with people. Unfortunately, most of the groups are used as a pure spam channel. People are 'shouting' by sharing their updates, but no one listens to them.

It takes time to find the appropriate group with high activity and strict rules that prevent spamming. If your target audience can be found on LinkedIn, then you definitely should give LinkedIn groups a try.

Step 1: Search for relevant groups on LinkedIn and join them. Make sure to try different keyword variations and use the group filters in the search settings.

Step 2: Once you're in, please don't start sharing your stuff right away. I know it's really tempting, but don't do it. Read the rules and scroll down to see how people interact in the group.

Step 3: If you think the group is not used as a pure spam channel and it's also allowed to share your own content, then give first by helping others, liking, commenting and even asking questions that move the conversation forward. Do it for a few weeks.

Step 4: After giving something to the community, it's time to share your own stuff. Don't just simply share your link. It's better to ask for feedback or opinions about a specific topic your content is about.

Note: The main goal of using LinkedIn groups is to get in touch with people who are interested in a specific topic. Use LinkedIn groups as a way to build your network and keep in touch with your target audience. Even if it's not an efficient promotional channel, you can still listen and engage with your audience.

Recommended reading:

5 Spam-Free Steps To Use LinkedIn Groups in Your Content Marketing Strategy

Top 10 Reasons To Start A LinkedIn Group

How to Network Using LinkedIn Groups

33. Write a teaser on LinkedIn

If your audience has a LinkedIn presence and uses it frequently, then you really should consider publishing articles on LinkedIn's platform. Once you have a great article on your blog, you should rewrite it in a shorter version and republish it on LinkedIn. Your network will be notified about your recent post and you can redirect them to your blog to continue reading there.

Step 1: Login to your LinkedIn account and select "Write an article".

Step 2: Once your post is published on your blog, write a 300-400 word teaser on LinkedIn.

Step 3: Make sure that you include links in the body of your post and at the bottom of the post so your readers can easily visit your website and read the original post. You can place a short call to action like this: "Click here to keep reading and to get some actionable tips!"

Don't just copy and paste text from your blog post. Instead, create an original post so you can avoid a duplicate content penalty from Google.

Recommended reading:

4 Ways to Write LinkedIn Posts That Turn Into Career Opportunities

6 Tips to Create and Publish a Killer Article on LinkedIn

How To Use LinkedIn Pulse To Drive Traffic And Subscribers To Your Blog

6 Tips for Writing Successful LinkedIn Articles

34. Google Plus Community hack

Google Plus isn't dead. Actually, it has 300 million active monthly users. It also offers some unique advantages over other social networks that enable blog owners to drive traffic to their websites.

Communities are the most valuable parts of Google Plus. Joining and taking part in conversations will get you more followers and engagement on the platform. All you need is just a small twist.

Step 1: Search for your niche keywords on Google Plus. Scroll down to the "Communities" section and click "More" to see all results.

Step 2: Join the communities and start building relationships with the members. Share your thoughts, answer questions and keep the conversation going.

Step 3: Get in touch with the owner of the community and ask her if she needs a hand. Matthew Barby did exactly this. He got approved as a moderator and received a huge spike in followers and engagement. Here is Matthew's pro tip:

Pro Tip: If your business page is a moderator on a Google+ community, all of the +1s from that community will be added to your business page. (And if that's linked to your website, it will pass on to your homepage!).

Recommended reading:

Why Google Plus is a Great Traffic Generation Source

Google Plus Communities – Complete User Guide

Become A Great Google Plus Community Member

35. Grow your Instagram followers

With this tactic, you can get 10K new followers for your Instagram account. All you need to do is to engage and follow other users.

Since Instagram doesn't allow third party apps to follow and unfollow others in large quantity, you have to do it manually. It takes a bit longer, but if you have some time during commuting and got tired of Candy Crush, it could be a pretty good time killer.

Step 1: Open Instagram and tap on the search icon and select "Tags" (you need to tap on the search label). Search the hashtag associated with your topic.

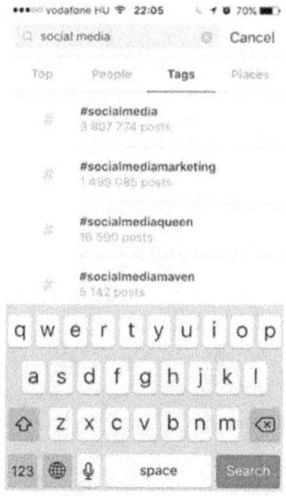

Step 2: Choose the top picture and follow the account.

Step 3: Go to the user's photos, and like their most recent three. Wait and see how people start following you back.

Recommended reading:

TOP 101 growth hacks - 2: The best new growth hacking ideas that INSPIRE you to put them into practice right away

36. Boost shares with locked content

Locking your content partly or completely could be a great way to get some extra social shares for your post. But it's a double-edged sword. I have seen great and also pretty bad results when we tried using this tactic. Sometimes it could increase social shares, sometimes you achieve exactly the opposite.

Locking your content means that it completely or partly won't be visible for your readers until they share it on social media. I suggest you only partly lock some parts of your article and try to hook your readers first. So chances will be higher that they will actually unlock that part since you already proved the value of your content.

Step 1: Add Social Locker plugin to your website. You can download it from here. If your blog runs on WordPress, then under the Plugin menu, search for "Social locker".

Step 2: After activating the plugin a dedicated section will be added to the left menu. Click "New Locker" to create a new one.

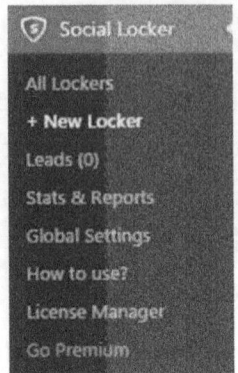

Step 3: Customize your settings and make sure to use "Manual locking". This feature allows you to partly lock your content.

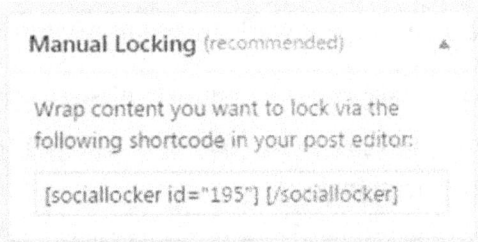

Step 4: After you finished editing your social locker, hit "Publish". Go to your blog post editor and wrap your content you would like to lock with the shortcodes. Make sure to switch to the text view.

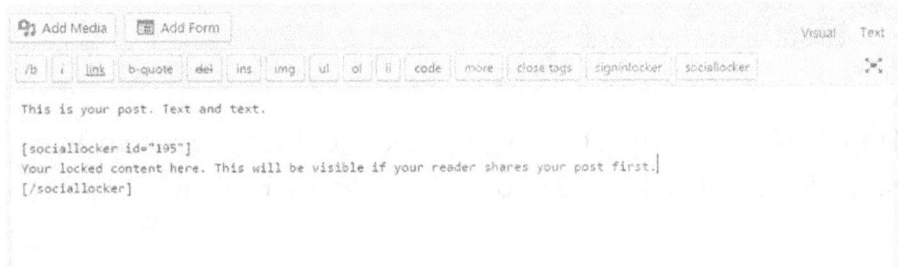

Step 5: Publish your article and measure if your readers start unlocking the hidden parts. Your readers will see something like this:

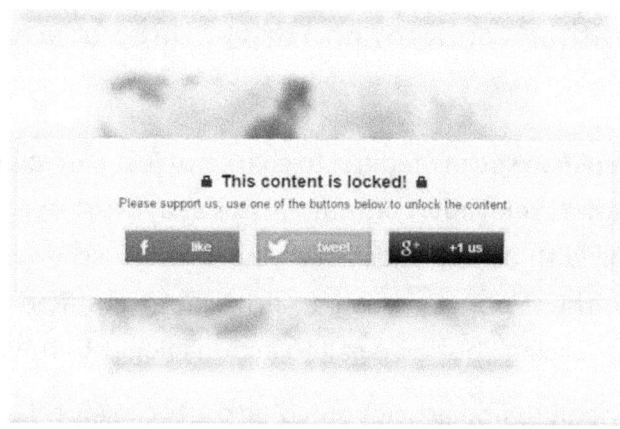

Recommended tools:

Social Locker

Recommended Reading:

5 Social Locker Plugins & Tools to Boost Your Blog's Social Signals

7 Quality Social Lockers for WordPress

How to Use OnePress Social Locker to Grow Your Social Media Following

37. Share other's content and drive traffic to your website

The golden rule on social media is to share not just your own content, but also other relevant content. This is a great way to build relationships with others and make your content schedule colorful. You can use these popular posts to drive some traffic back to your own blog by placing your own call to action widget to their website.

Step 1: We need to find articles and blog posts closely related to your already published post. Select a keyword that best describes your post, for example: "content promotion tips" and use Google Alerts or Mention to track that keyword and get notified when a new article containing the keyword is published.

Step 2: Once you found an article your audience probably likes, use Sniply to share it on your social channels. Go to Sniply's website to register a free account.

Step 3: Insert the article's link where you would like to get traffic from and hit "Create snip". Customize the call-to-action (CTA) visitors who clicked on your Sniply link will see. Make sure that you're linking to your post.

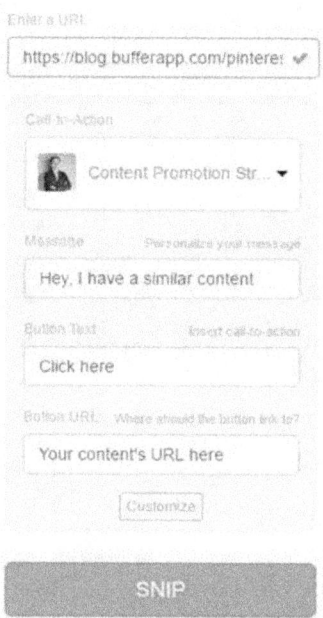

Step 4: Click "Snip" and we're all set! It should look like this (with a more creative text).

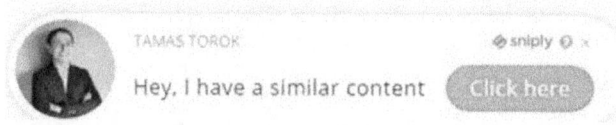

See how people engage with your post and your call to action. You should see people clicking on your CTA and landing on your website.

Tools:

Google Alerts

Mention

Sniply

Recommended reading:

How I use Sniply to get Quality Traffic

Share Content and Drive Traffic to Your Site with Sniply

Content Curation and Web Traffic with Sniply

38. Easily double your social traffic

You just finished your brand new post and you're excited to share it on social media with your followers. But how many times do you share the same post? Once? Twice?

The thing is, if you don't share your links a few times, then only a fraction of your followers will see it. By sharing the same post more than once at different times, you can reach a much broader audience and even double your current social traffic. This is a pretty simple and really powerful strategy and if you do it smart, your followers won't see it as spamming.

Step 1: Create different post variations for the link you would like to share multiple times. Around 7-10 variations are good enough. See tip 6 for crafting catchy headlines.

Step 2: Set up the sharing schedule in advance by using Buffer. Marketers at Coschedule used the following schedule: shared the article right after it was published, 1 hour later, 3 hours later, next day, next week, next month and two months after the publication.

Step 3: See how your posts perform and feel free to adjust your schedule to your audience's activity.

Pro tip: Apart from changing the titles of your posts, try to use different pictures, hashtags and even emojis to boost engagement.

Tools:

Buffer

CoSchedule

Recommended reading:

How to Easily Double Your Traffic from Social Media

Social Media Strategy: How Much Time Does a Good Strategy Really Take?

Why We Sent a Single Tweet 44 Times

39. Extra shares by mentioning additional resources

It's pretty easy to get some extra shares by mentioning others' work in your content. There are two ways you can do that. First, by using them as a reference in your post's body or creating a dedicated "additional reading" section in your blog post.

Step 1: Search for popular articles related to your new content. Try to find 5-6 additional articles, blog posts, podcasts or videos. Every format is perfect if it provides additional value to your reader. You can use tools like Buzzsumo to find the most shared content for a specific keyword.

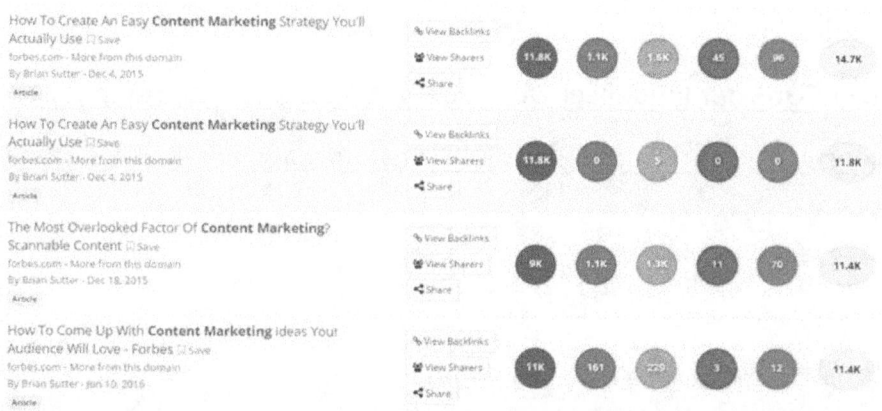

Step 2: Get in touch with them early. Let them know you're writing new content and will include their work in your post. Ask permission if they would like to see the post once you're done. By following this method, you won't just appear out of the blue and ask them to share your post. In this case, you start with relationship building by mentioning their work and linking back to their website.

Step 3: As soon as your article is out, shoot them an email letting them know that they're featured in your newly published post. You can even notify those who haven't replied to your email in Step 3 (maybe they just had a busy week).

Step 4: If they like your content then some of them will automatically share it on social media. Otherwise, ask them kindly if they could help you with a share.

Tools:

Buzzsumo

Recommended reading:

How To Create a Killer Outreach Email With 4 Quick Steps and 3 Simple Tips

Power Up Your Influencer Outreach with These 2 Email Templates

Blogger Outreach Tips: How To Write Outreach Emails That Don't Suck

40. Extra social shares from newsletter

Collecting emails from your visitors is still one of the most important things you should focus on. Email is still the most powerful way to get and keep in touch with your readers.

In this tip I'm showing you how you can get some extra social shares and traffic for your blog post by using social share call to actions in your newsletter.

Step 1: First, you need to know what social channels your readers use the most. Go to Google Analytics and from the menu on the left side, select "Acquisition" and under the "All traffic" section, click "Source/Medium". Set a 3-4 month date range and you will see the most relevant social channels that drive traffic to your blog.

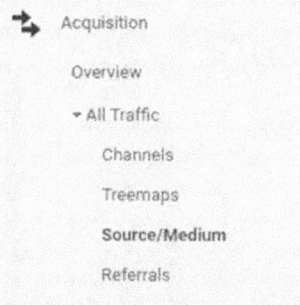

Step 2: Add a short call to action to your email and ask your subscribers to share that piece of content with others. I recommend you put this call to action to the end of your email (as a PS).

Step 3: To make this sharing process as smooth as possible, you should write to their social platform to update for them. I like to use Share Link Generator for this, which makes it super easy to create Facebook, Twitter, Google Plus, Pinterest and LinkedIn updates in advance.

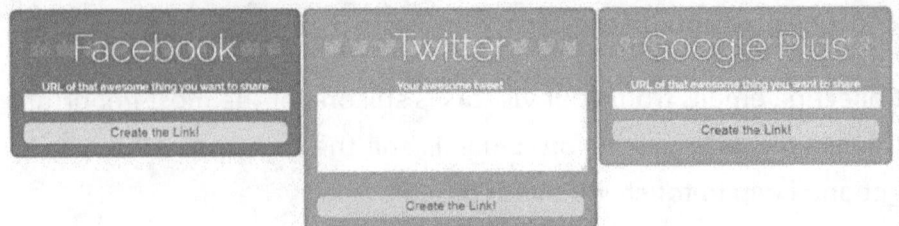

Your readers will be able to share your blog post with two clicks.

Tools:

Share Link Generator

Click to tweet

Recommended reading:

75 calls to action to use in your email marketing campaigns

7 Tips for a Powerful Email Call to Action

Call to Action Phrases That Will Convert

41. Less is more

It's quite obvious that you have to add share buttons to your blog posts. Websites without social buttons feel like they are still living in the pre-social media era. But just adding random share buttons or embedding all the possible options may not the best idea.

Sure, you have to use social buttons, but which one and how many of them? Is there an optimal number?

Step 1: You need to look at your website's analytics to see what actually happens there. If you use Google Analytics, from the left menu, click on "Acquisition" and under "All traffic", select "Source/ Medium". Set the date range for a few months and see which social channels drive the most and best quality visitors.

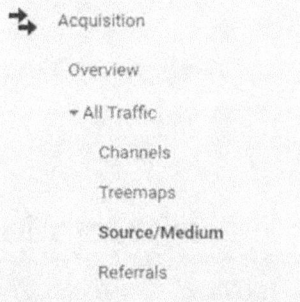

Step 2: You should also check out the demographic data of your audience. In Google Analytics, you can find more information under the "Audience" menu (you need to enable this feature). Or you can use Quantcast, which is a tool for audience measurement. Register for free and add its code to your website's head section. You need to wait a bit until it collects enough data to show.

Step 3: Actually, too many share buttons could do more harm than good. They could slow down your page, which makes your search engine ranking worse. Also, according to a psychological study, too many options can hinder decision making.

Step 4: I'm sure now you have a list of 3-4 social channels that are responsible for the majority of your social traffic. Make sure to add these share buttons to your website. If you're targeting younger generations then it might be worth experimenting with WhatsApp and Facebook Messenger share buttons. Since 70% of social sharing takes place in private channels, such as email, chat and messaging apps, it hides a huge potential. AddThis allows you to add WhatsApp and Facebook Messenger to your share buttons.

Tools:

Google Analytics

Quantcast

AddThis

Recommended reading:

Too Many Social Media Sharing Buttons Make Your Site Less Social

70% Of Social Sharing Is Mobile, Private And Absent From Your Business' Data

What Is The Best Placement For Successful Social Media Buttons?

7 Secrets For Crazy Clickable Social Media Buttons

42. Use social proof to get more shares

You see two restaurants on the street, one with a huge crowd queuing up on the street and another one with nobody inside. In this case, we automatically assume that the food must be very good at the crowded place and pretty bad at the empty one. When we decide between these restaurants, we tend to choose the one with social proof.

Social proof is a powerful way to fuel your content marketing efforts and it can be used to get more shares for your blog post.

Step 1: In your social buttons' settings, find the option where you can turn on the share counter. This will show your readers how many people shared your content. If you don't have that option you could replace your share buttons with AddThis or ShareThis.

Step 2: In certain plugins, you can set up a threshold for this counter, so it won't show big zero shares until the number of shares reaches a certain limit. Save the settings and see if it makes the difference.

Tools:

AddThis

ShareThis

Recommended reading:

Displaying Social Proof – What the Marketing Experts Use

Social Proof: Your Key to More Magnetic Marketing

The Science of Social Proof: 5 Types and the Psychology Behind Why They Work

43. Inspire your audience to share

It's already a big thing when you successfully drive traffic to your blog post and social sharing is like icing on the cake. We like it and it's great to attract more visitors. But it's not easy to convince readers to share your stuff; most of them won't share it even if they like what you created.

But if they really like your stuff, then they probably want to read more. I recommend you offer an incentive to share your content. It could be an extra worksheet, a PDF, a template or some really useful bonus tip they can get in exchange.

Step 1: Register a free Pay with a tweet account. It checks if someone shared your content and makes sure to deliver your giveaway.

Step 2: Create a new campaign and carefully customize every part of it. Add your title, allowed networks (Facebook, Twitter, LinkedIn, Google Plus can be selected) and make sure you link to the bonus content.

Step 3: You will get a campaign-button or plain campaign link to integrate into your page. Copy the code and insert it where you want it to appear. Once someone clicks on the button, it will tell your reader that they will get the bonus stuff if they share the current content.

Tools:

Pay with a like

Pay with a tweet

Recommended reading:

Pay With a Tweet vs. Pay With an Email [Case Study with Infographic]

How to Use "Pay With a Tweet" to Generate Leads

5 Proven Social Media Call-to-Action Tips [Research]

44. Create roundup posts

Roundup posts are collections of content in a given topic within a certain period of time. You can see bloggers who curate content this way by simply creating monthly or weekly collections of great content related to their topic. The most important reason for creating roundup posts is to get extra shares on social media from the authors of the featured articles.

Step 1: You need to find the newest and greatest content to include in your weekly or monthly roundups. There are several ways to do it:

- RSS-based notification: I recommend you use Feedly, which collects every new post from blogs you subscribed to via RSS.

- Subscribe to relevant blogs to get notified about the latest updates.

- Set up keyword trackers, such as Google Alerts or Mention, to track every single post containing your keywords.

Step 2: Put your selected articles into a blog post and write a few sentences of introduction for each one. Make sure you link back to the original source.

Step 3: I recommend you notify your sources before you publish your post. Just let them know you're working on a roundup post and their article will be included. The goal of this step is just to give a quick heads up. To get their email address, check out tip 11.

Step 4: Run your outreach campaign and schedule automatic follow up emails (after 3-4 days from your first email), just in case your email gets buried in their mailbox. My favorite tool is Contentmarketer.io, but you can also use a free Excel scheduler (YAMM) for sending a smaller amount of emails.

Tools:

Contentmarketer.io

YAMM

Feedly

Mention

Google Alerts

Recommended reading:

How to Curate a Roundup Blog Post of Industry Influencers

How to create an expert roundup blog post

The Ultimate Guide To Link Roundup Posts

45. Influencer roundups

Involving influencers in your content promotion efforts could significantly boost your reach on social media. If you create something epic, something that stands out, and provides a new perspective, chances are that your selected influencers will also share it with their followers. But you know, we can't just appear out of the blue and ask a bunch of influencers to share your stuff. 99% of the time, it won't work. At tip 10, you can read more about how to start building relationships with influencers.

In this tip, I'm highlighting one method I have been using and it worked pretty well for me: influencer roundup interviews.

Step 1: Identify the topic you would like to ask influencers about. Try to find one simple question that your audience often asks and wants to learn more about.

Step 2: Once you know what you want to ask, search for the influencers you would like to include in your interview post. You can use Buzzsumo for finding them and you can also check Klout for more info.

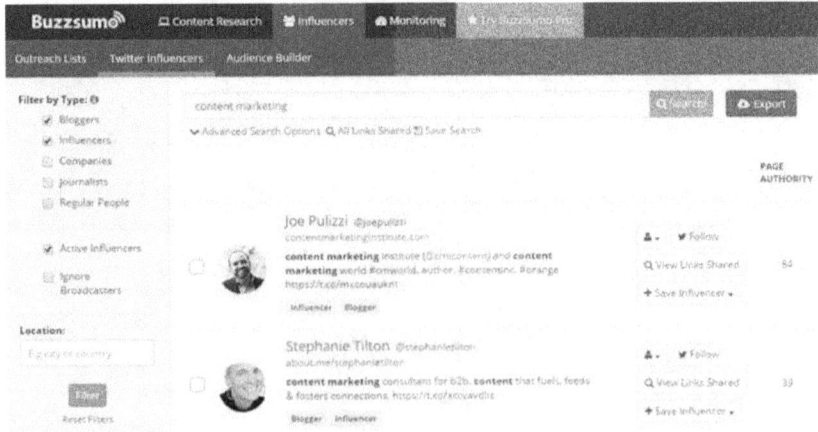

Step 3: Get in touch with them and keep your message super short and right to the point. Let them know that you're working on an expert roundup and would like to include them in the post. I'm sure most of them will be happy to help.

Step 4: Before you publish your expert roundup post, reach out to your influencers and ask their feedback on your piece. Make the necessary changes before you're ready to publish it.

Step 5: After publication, send another email to the featured influencers and let them know that your article went live. If they like what you did, then they will share it with their followers. Don't be too pushy begging for shares. It could easily ruin your relationship in this early stage.

Tools:

Buzzsumo

Klout

Recommended reading:

How to Write an Expert RoundUp Post the Right Way

7 Ways To Make Your Next Expert Roundup Stand Out

How to Interview Influencers (Even If You'd Rather Curl up and Die)

46. Promote different parts of your blog post

You have a list post with some great tips, but instead of promoting the whole article on social media, you can simply promote only a part of it by using jump links.

These links allow the readers to jump to different parts of your article. You can use it to help them navigate within your post and also to share a jump link on social media so when someone visits your site, they will start reading your post from a specific part.

Since only a fraction of your followers will see your original post about your latest article, you should share your article several times to get higher reach. Jump links do a really great job here, since you can slice up your long list post and share each tip separately but still direct visitors to the same article.

Step 1: Give each tip in your list a name, such as tip_one (use underscore instead of spaces).

Step 2: Insert the name of each tip between the following HTML tag: <a id="tip_one">

Step 3: Replace the section's title you would like to link to. It should look like this:

<a id="tip_one">The title of your tip</a>

Step 4: Create a link that will take the reader to the selected object: <a href="#tip_one">Click here to see tip one</a>. You can place these links at the beginning of your articles so other visitors can jump to the part they want to read. It should look like this:

Jump right to the tips:

- 1. Increase social media traffic by placing share buttons on your thank you page
- 2. Add share buttons to your PDF document
- 3. Insert shareable quotes to your guide
- 4. Hide bonus content in your guide (Pay with a share)

Step 5: Create a new social media update for each tip and use the link pointing to that specific tip. Here is an example: *www.yourwebsite.com/your-article-lin#tip1*. You can use Buffer or Edgar to schedule your updates in advance.

Step 6: Create awesome visuals for each tip, so they will look different when you share them on social media. I recommend you use Canva or check out the free sources at tip 9.

Tools:

Buffer

Edgar

Canva

Recommended reading:

How to Create a Link to Jump to a Specific Part of a Page [Quick Tip]

How to Create Stunning Social Media Graphics WITHOUT Photoshop

Creating Easy Branded Images for Your Blog and Social Media

47. Encourage private sharing

WhatsApp and Facebook Messenger are the most popular instant messaging apps in the world.

In terms of usage, the statistics are impressive; 55% of global internet users use instant messaging apps every day and private messaging offers immediate reception and open rates could be as high as 70%. It's a growing communication channel with insane engagement. In this tip, I'm showing you how you can use instant messaging to get extra traffic to your blog. It's a pretty good way to entice your mobile visitors to share your content.

Step 1: We need to look into the data to see if it's worth the effort. In Google Analytics under the "Audience" menu, select "Mobile" to see the proportion of mobile traffic.

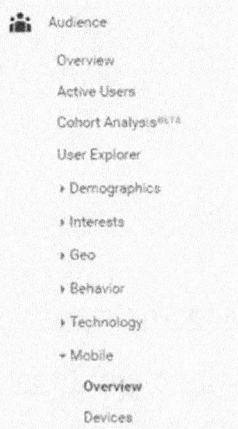

Step 2: We should show different share buttons to those who are visiting your website on desktop and on mobile. In case of mobile visitors, we're going to pay more attention to instant messaging. Go to Addthis.com to get started.

Step 3: Select "Tools" from the menu and click "Create new". First we create share buttons for mobile visitors. In the settings, make

103

sure to set desktop to "hide" and mobile to "bottom". Manually customize it and add the preferred instant messaging apps to the list.

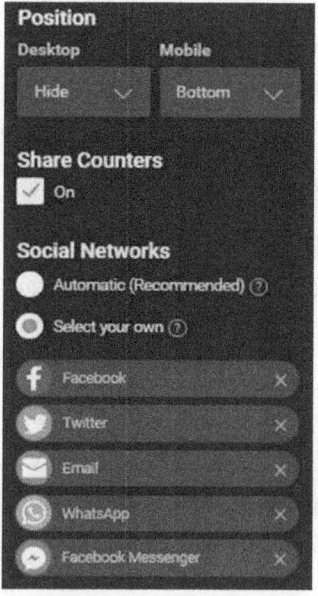

Step 4: Hit "Save and continue" and we're all set.

Tools:

Addthis

Google Analytics

Recommended reading:

The Rise Of Instant Messengers: 5 Ways To Do Marketing With Instant Messaging

WhatsApp is the world's most popular messaging app on Android, says report

48. Get more shares with interactive content

Everyone likes having fun and most people get excited to know more about their personality or revealing their Native Indian and rock star name. You can use similar tactics to generate more shares for your content and also keep your visitors longer on your website.

Fortunately, creating quizzes is not a rocket science. They are easy to use. Drag and drop editors are out there so you don't need any programming skills to create your own quizzes or personality tests.

Step 1: To create your own quiz, register a free account at apester.com.

Step 2: After registration, click "Create New" and select the type of interactive content you would like to create.

Step 3: Add your questions and mark the right answers. Carefully select visuals, it has to look gorgeous. If you're not a Photoshop ninja, you can use a drag and drop visual editor such as Canva.

Step 4: Hit "Publish" and if your blog runs on Wordpress, install Apester's plugin.

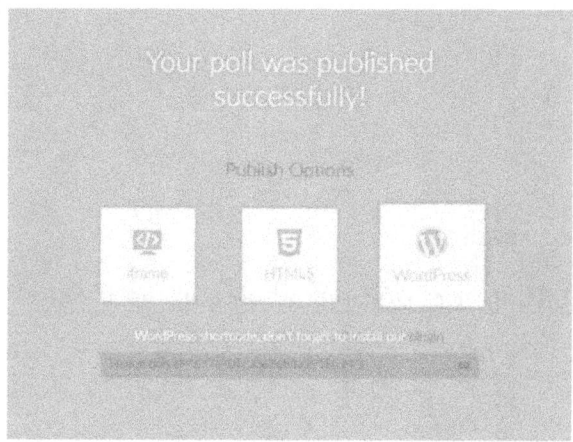

Step 5: Copy the code and insert it anywhere on your website you want it to appear.

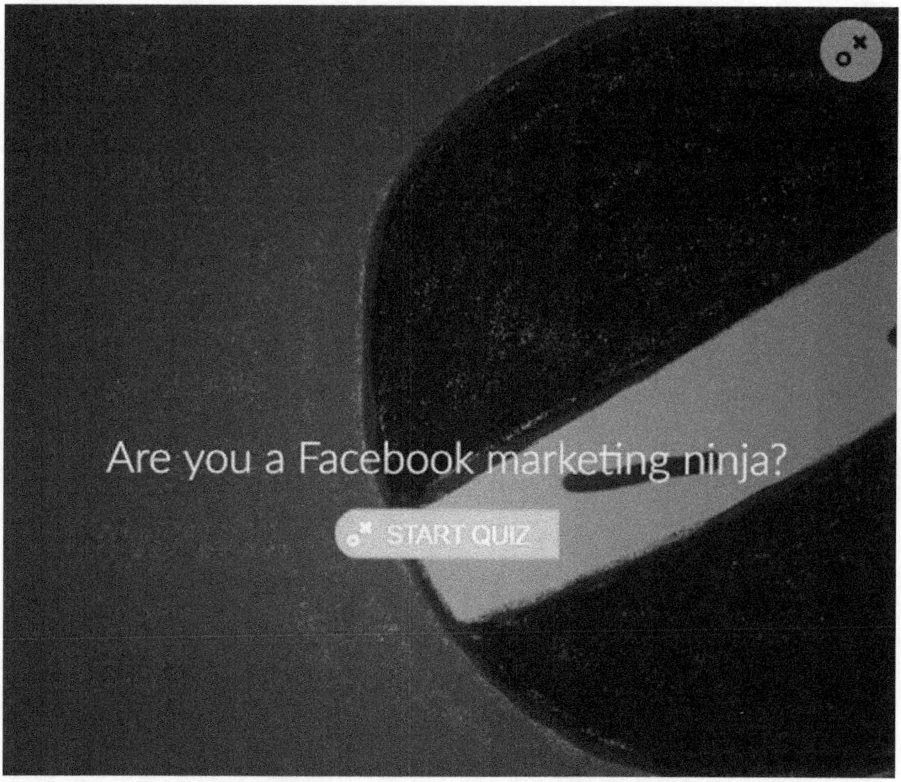

![Are you a Facebook marketing ninja? START QUIZ]

Tools:

Apester

Canva

Recommended reading:

10 Useful web tools for creating online quizzes and polls

The Marketer's Guide to Using Quizzes to Reach and Engage Your Audience

These 3 Tips Will Help You Make Engaging Quizzes

49. Find people who have linked to similar content

In this tip, we're looking for people who have linked to an article similar to your newly published one.

Since they linked out to a similar article, they might be interested in your post as well. In this case, we aren't asking to replace that other link with your new one. We get in touch to get their feedback on our stuff and, if appropriate, ask for a share.

Step 1: Find popular content related to your new content. I like to use Buzzsumo to see the most shared content for specific keywords. Register or log in to Buzzsumo and search for your keyword that best describes your post.

Step 2: From the results, you can see the most shared articles on your topic. Click on the "View backlinks" button to see who linked to these articles. Another way to do it is simply copy the article links and insert them to Open Site Explorer.

Step 3: Create a list of these websites in an Excel sheet and make sure to add the contact details of the author. Read tip 11 on how to find almost anyone's email address.

Step 4: Let them know that you just created a similar, updated version of the content they previously linked to. Ask for their thoughts on your content first. Once they get back to you with a positive answer, you could ask them to share it on social media.

Tools:

Open Site Explorer

Buzzsumo

Recommended reading:

9 Free Backlink Checker Tools To Check Competitors Backlinks

8 Actionable Ways To Get Backlinks By Spying On Your Competitors

50. Run a contest for sharing

Creating contests on social media is a great way to blow up engagement, get more traffic and subscribers to your blog.

But you need to be careful with the incentives you offer in your social media contest.

A few years ago, I read a case study about a social media contest ran by a tractor dealer on Facebook. They wanted to get more likes for their Facebook page so they started a contest where everyone can take part by liking their page and a lucky one will win an iPad.

And this is where things went terribly wrong. They got new followers, but most of them just came for the free bounty and weren't interested in the company's products. So this tractor dealer just bought zombie followers, no engagement, no new sales.

The problem here was the misfit between the reward and the company's target. When you create your own contest, make sure to offer something that attracts your target audience. Otherwise, you're just collecting zombie followers for your social media account.

In this tip, I'm showing you how to create a contest on social media that will engage your target audience.

Step 1: Sign up for Rafflecopter. Rafflecopter makes it "mega simple" to launch and manage a giveaway for any brand, on any website.

Step 2: Click "New giveaway" and first add a prize your winner(s) will receive.

Gift Card for 250 RaflCoin

For example: " 2 Superbowl Tickets "

+ ADD AN IMAGE

CANCEL   SAVE THIS PRIZE   >

Step 3: Add the ways people can take part in the contest. You can choose many different options, such as visiting a fan page, tweeting a message or subscribing to a newsletter. For each option, you can set points people will receive. The more they get, the higher their chances will be to win. Set up the start and end date of the campaigns and hit "Preview & Install".

People can enter by...

Referring their friends (aka. "viral sharing")   ?

+ ADD AN ENTRY OPTION

It starts...   ...and ends

10/25/2016   11/01/2016

12:00 ▼   AM ▼   12:00 ▼   AM ▼

Times are in Eastern Time (US & Canada) — CHANGE

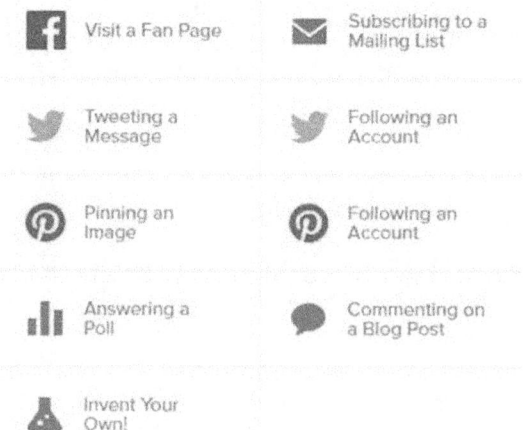

Step 4: You can embed it in your website or run it on your Facebook page. In the premium version, you have more options to customize your contest.

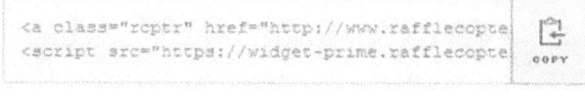

Tools:

Rafflecopter

Recommended reading:

11 Simple Steps For Successful Social Media Giveaways

How To Run A Successful Blog Giveaway

How to Run a Simple Contest and Add 500 New Subscribers to Your List

51. Social shares from your favorite tools

If you're creating super actionable content for your readers then this tip is for you.

When describing something in greater detail, you probably use tools to show your readers every single step they should take to execute your idea. Just look at this book. For every tip, I added a tool section, containing tools I used or recommend to use to implement a tactic. This is a great way to get some extra shares on social media while you help these tools to get new users. It's really a win-win for both of you.

Step 1: Try to find the email address of the founder or someone who's responsible for that product. To find anyone's email address check out tip 11.

Step 2: Ping them before your article is published, let them know that in your newest post, you will be featuring their tool. Ask them if they want to get a quick heads up when it goes live.

Step 3: Notify them once your article is published and kindly ask them to share it with their followers.

Recommended reading:

Reaching out without creeping out: Your 101 guide to building your network online

Perfect email

How to Craft the Perfect Outreach Email

52. Social traffic from images

Using great visuals in your post will not only make your content easier to read and understand but will also provide a great way to get some extra shares for that post. SumoMe's Image Sharer makes it easier for your visitors to share images from your website with a link back to your articles. This tool works especially well with images that trigger emotions, which could be informative charts, funny images or a picture of a cute puppy. You get the concept.

Step 1: Register at Sumome.com. You should copy and paste SumoMe's code to the <head> section of your website. If your blog is running on Wordpress, then there is a free plugin that helps you easily edit your website's header and footer.

Step 2: On your website's left or right side, you should see a small toolbar with the SumoMe icon. From the tool menu, select the Image Sharer app and add to your website.

Step 3: Choose up to five services to share images and customize the position, design and display rules of the buttons. Here is an example of how it should look (see the bottom right corner):

Tools:

Sumome Image Sharer

Insert Headers and Footers (plugin)

Recommended reading:

How to Create Engaging Images for Social Media: A Simple Guide For Non-Designers

How to Create Engaging Images for Social Media

6 Types of Images Guaranteed to Enhance Your Blog's Content

53. The perfect image for your social media post

Visual content process information 60.000X faster in the brain than text. And 65% of people are visual learners, so it's no wonder that most of us love images. According to Canva Design School, the following image types are the most appropriate for Facebook posts:

- **Photos**: relevant, everyday photos of products
- **Charts**: simple, informative charts
- **Visual representations**: for explaining complex things
- **Comics**: everybody likes having fun and it also triggers positive emotions
- **Annotated Screenshots**: a great screenshot is a good way to show, instead of tell

When choosing an image for your blog post, **try to avoid using lame stock photos** such as ones that illustrate people with fake emotions in unimaginable situations. Instead, try finding high-quality stock photos; see tip 9 for a list.

What colors do men and women prefer?

The **most popular colors** among men are blue (57%), green (14%) and black (9%). Interestingly, women's number one favorite color is blue (35%), followed by purple (23%) and green (14%).

The **least favorite colors** among men are brown (27%), orange (22%) and purple (22%). Women's least favorite colors are orange (33%), brown (20%) and grey (17%).

If you are targeting an audience of mostly women or men, make sure to have a look at the preferred colors. This preference list provides a good base to start to run your own experiments. You can even ask your target audience about their color preferences. Probably, this is the most practical solution.

Tools:

Canva

Pablo

Recommended reading:

Top 40 Most Engaging Images on Facebook by Top Brands

How to Create Facebook Image Posts That Engage

How to Fully Engage Your Readers' Brains with Images [SlideShare]

54. Traffic from your sources

When we write a blog post, we often use resources and other posts to support our arguments. It's not just good for making your points more authentic, but also a great opportunity to get some traffic from these sources. Make sure you start this process before your article is published.

Step 1: Create a list of resources you used in your blog post. I like to put everything in an Excel sheet with the following columns: article link, title, author name, author email.

Step 2: Research the email address of the author or simply fill out the contact form on her blog. For more details on researching their email addresses, check out tip 11.

Step 3: Reach out to your resources before your blog post is published. Let them know that you used their work in your post and nicely ask for a feedback. Some of them will get back to you with their suggestions.

This approach is good for two reasons: 1. You build a relationship with them and 2. You involve them in creating your blog post so when you are ready, they will more likely reply and help you with promotion.

Step 4: When your blog post is published, notify them. Thank them again for their help and, if appropriate, ask them to share it with their followers.

Pro tip: You can also send out an email for those who haven't replied to your first message. Maybe they just got busy and your message was buried in their mailbox. Only ask for feedback in the email, don't ask for a share directly.

Tools:

Contentmarketer.io

Recommended reading:

How to find anyone's email address

The Complete Guide To Finding Any Email Address: Tools, Tips, Tactics, And More

11 Email Experiments + the Citation Labs Outreach Best Practices Record

Part 5: Organic and Referral Traffic

Search engine optimization is what every content marketer should keep in mind. This section consists of many white hat SEO tips that actually work. You will see step-by-step instructions on link building, on site SEO and keyword research to outrank your competitors and get more organic traffic to your website.

55. Get interviews from high authority sites

Did you know that there are hundreds of reporters out there looking for expert advice? If you're good enough, you can be featured on big sites like *Wall Street Journal* and *Forbes* with a link pointing back to your blog. A link or citation (mention of your brand) from a high authority site will boost your domain authority score so you will be ranking better in Google search and you can also expect to get a traffic boost in the short term.

All you need to do is to prove that you're an authentic expert in your field and provide a really valuable answer to them. Just follow these steps:

Step 1: Register at HARO.com (Help a Reporter Out) and don't forget to select the most appropriate fields you would like to receive questions on.

Step 2: You will receive three emails every single day containing a list of queries reporters are searching for more information about. Scan these emails and find the ones that are relevant to your field.

Step 3: Make sure you don't waste your time; before you start answering a question, check the domain authority score of the website where you are expecting your answer to appear. Use CheckMoz for this quick check.

121

Pro tip: You can improve your credibility by making sure that your website looks good and contains really great posts to show.

Tools:

MyBlogU

Haro

Checkmoz

Small SEO Tools

Recommended reading:

How to Get Interviewed by Popular Blogs (Even If You're Not a Big Shot)

How to Land Big Interviews When Your Blog is Still Small

How to Get Interviewed 200 Times a year For Your Blog

56. Easy way to get backlinks and referral traffic

If you're waiting to get some backlinks organically from other bloggers then you should stop dreaming and start being proactive to speed up the process. You need to show that you exist, otherwise, chances are they won't even hear about you.

A relatively fast way to get links to your blog is through roundup blog posts. These are collections of interesting articles, linking back to the original source (to your blog) created by a fellow blogger.

Step 1: Search for blogs that are creating roundup posts. Since we're looking for active roundup bloggers, make sure you set the search filter on Google for the past 1-2 months. Use the following search queries to find them:

- Your keyword + "recommended links"/"suggested links"
- Your keyword + "useful links"/"interesting links"
- Your keyword + "favorite links"
- Your keyword + "intitle:resources"
- Your keyword + "round up"
- Your keyword + "intitle: round up"
- Your keyword + "round up" + intitle:weekly/daily/monthly
- Your keyword + intitle:list
- Your keyword + "guide"

Step 2: Put the blogs into a list with the contact details of the author/owner. To find their email addresses, check tip 11 for some actionable ideas.

Step 3: Once you have a valid address, it's time to start building a relationship with them. You can first follow them on social media, share their stuff and also provide feedback on their content.

Step 4: The next step is to craft an email and ask them if they could include your post in their next roundup post. Mention that you're happy to share their next roundup post once it's published. You can also recommend other's article for the roundup post, so this way you won't seem that selfish. If you want to learn more about how to create an effective outreach campaign, check out tip 10.

Tools:

Contentmarketer.io

Recommended reading:

How to find anyone's email address

The Complete Guide To Finding Any Email Address: Tools, Tips, Tactics, And More

Find Email Addresses – 60+ Tools and Tips to Find Someone's Email

57. Links from your favorite tools

I'm sure you can mention several tools you can't live without. Believe it or not, this is a great opportunity to get some backlinks from these tools pointing to your website. All you need to do is to write a meaningful testimonial for these tools.

This tactic works especially well with new tools since they don't really have a big follower base and they're probably hungry for social proof.

Step 1: Collect all the tools you're using and create a list in a spreadsheet.

Step 2: Search for the contact details of these tools. Apart from getting a general email address, it might be worth taking the time and finding the contact details of the founders. Tip 11 shows you some tricks how to do it.

Step 3: Craft your pitch, tailored to every tool. Emphasize how it helped you save time, money or just simply made your life better.

Step 4: Send the testimonials to the contacts you have found. In the email, mention that you're a big fan and this is how you would like to give something back for their incredible work. Give them permission to use this anywhere they want. Also, attach your website address to your testimonial as proof you're a real person.

If they like your testimonial and can use it as an advantage on their website, then they will probably feature it. Your name and website's name will appear there with a link back to your website. You just got a new backlink!

Recommended reading:

11 Testimonial Page Examples You'll Want to Copy

How to Write Powerful Testimonials: 4 Simple Tips to Snatch More Clients

Your Guide To The Nine Types Of Testimonials (w/Examples)

58. Outrank everyone

People visit websites to find answers to their questions and you create content because you want to provide valuable information to them. In this game, you're competing against thousands of blogs. It's not only hard to grab your target audience's attention but also difficult to outrank your competitors on Google. If you can out-teach your competition then you will win and content hubs are great for that.

But what is a content hub?

A content hub is a set of content (usually web pages) organized around a specific topic (usually a central page). It could be a category on a blog or a section of pages on a website.

It is an organized structure of diverse assets in various content formats.

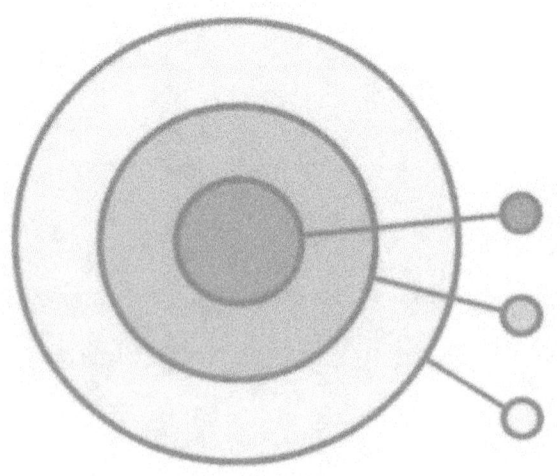

Content Hub Structure: Organization

CENTRAL HUB
Main topic, most competitive keyphrase

RELATED SUB-TOPICS
Answers to the main questions, "how to"

SUPPORTIVE BASE
Helpful info on broader range of related topics

Content hubs work because Google is getting smarter. It focuses less on key phrases and more on meaning. A content hub also helps people to easily dig deeper and learn more about a topic.

We know that building a stream of organic traffic takes time and this tactic definitely supports your efforts.

I heard about content hubs from Andy Crestodina when I did an interview with him a year ago. It's a pretty smart way to give a boost to your organic traffic. Instead of jumping from topic to topic, you need to be focused and need a structure (a content hub). All you need to do is a bit of research and strategic thinking around your content production.

Results? You should see a steady flow of organic traffic in the long term.

Step 1: You need to find a topic that is relevant to your target audience. Talk to them and try to discover their pain points, interests and needs around your topic. See how you can connect these to your website's ultimate goal.

Step 2: Check your competition. Use Buzzsumo to see the most shared content for that topic and do some Google searches to reveal who you are competing with. Check the top 10-20 results and discover their strong and weak points.

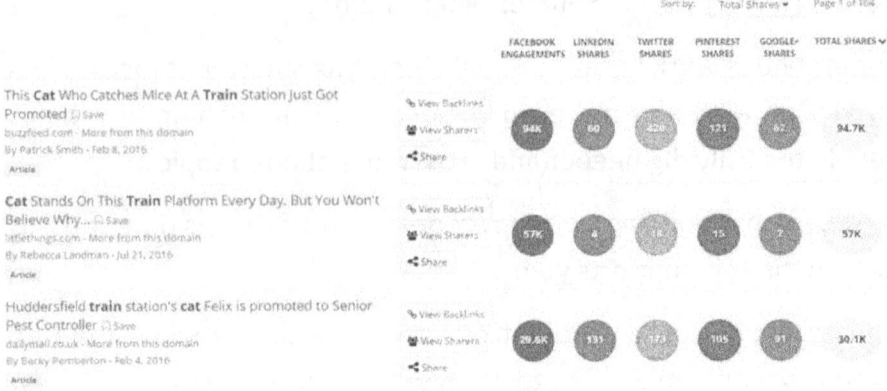

Step 3: Create the central part of the hub, focusing on a competitive key phrase. This has to be your strongest and most useful piece of content on your topic. Really, make it 10X better than your competitors. Check out the bonus package for some tips.

Step 4: Build supportive content around your central content. Each piece of content you create should have its own key phrase that is a subtopic of the central content. For example, if you write about social media promotion as a central content, your subtopic could be content about social media outreach tools. Make sure to link this supportive content to the central content.

Tools

Buzzsumo

Recommended reading:

Content Hubs: How to Beat the Big Boys in 7 Steps

59. Target group of keywords

If you want to get organic traffic to your blog post, first you need to decide what keywords you want to rank for. But instead of focusing on keywords with huge traffic, find long tail keywords with much lower search queries but also much lower competition.

Google is getting smarter and smarter every year. Search engines have changed a lot and they don't just focus on key phrases, but also the overall meaning of your content. You have to create content that covers the general meaning to get better ranking and more organic traffic.

Step 1: We need to find a long tail keyword that's going to be the focus keyword of your article. This is the keyword you want to rank for. Go to Keyword Planner and search for general keywords that best describe your blog post.

Keyword Planner
Where would you like to start?

Q Find new keywords and get search volume data

▸ Search for new keywords using a phrase, website or category

▸ Get search volume data and trends

▸ Multiply keyword lists to get new keywords

Under the "variations" tab, find other keywords that might be worth focusing on. From the list, select the one with low competition and low traffic so your content can be more competitive for that niche keyword.

cat punishment techniques	10 – 100	Low
top cat training	10 – 100	Low
what can you teach a cat	10 – 100	Low
how to teach your cat to play dead	10 – 100	Low
how is your cat	10 – 100	Low
can cats learn	10 – 100	Low
things you can train your cat to do	10 – 100	Low

Select your focus keyword from this list.

Step 2: You need to figure out which phrases are semantically linked in Google. Search for your selected focus keyword (from the previous step) and scroll down to the bottom of the page. Check the "related searches" to see exactly what Google considered as connected phrases.

Searches related to what can you teach a cat

cat tricks youtube	cat exam tricks
cat trick hearthstone	list of cat tricks
easy tricks to teach your cat	cat trick hs
how to teach your cat to sit	funny cat tricks

Step 3: Select the ones that are the closest to your topic and perform a search for each. Scroll down again and see the related searches for that keyword. Continue it until you have a solid list.

Step 4: If you want your content to be considered as the best content of the internet in that topic, make sure to include as many keywords as possible from the suggestions of related searches. But instead of just stuffing them into your post, work it out to fit them naturally in your content.

You really have to create the best possible content for that topic. How do you do that? Check out tip 5 and 7 and the bonus resources for some ideas

Pro tip: To get your content indexed faster and open the flow of organic traffic, visit Pingomatic.com to ping search engines. It takes just a minute to fill out the necessary information and within a few hours your freshly published content will be visible in the search results.

Tools:

Keyword Planner

Search engine pinger

Recommended reading:

SEO 101: What is Semantic Search and Why Should I Care?

Top 7 Semantic Search Engines as an Alternative to Google

Everything You Need To Know About Semantic Search And What It Means for Your Website

60. Use the Skyscraper technique

The skyscraper technique was created and popularized by Brian Dean. Brian was able to generate 300 thousand referral visitors with this technique. The genius lies in its simplicity. It's a three step process and all you need to do is to find link-worthy content and make it even better, at least 10X better.

If you implement this tip, you will be able to get more links for your content that will drive you more referral and organic traffic.

Step 1: You need to find linkable content that has already proved their value and usefulness. You can simply do a Google search for your selected keywords and see the top content for that keyword.

If you know your competitor(s) then use OpenLinkProfiler to see their most linked content. Go to OpenLinkProfiler and paste the URL of your competitor's website.

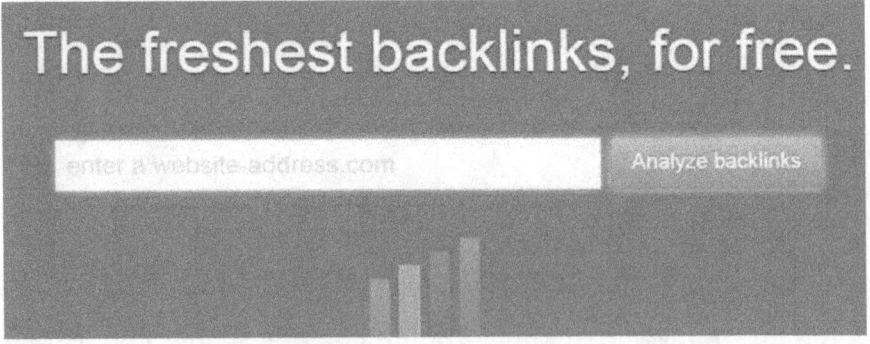

From the left menu, select "Pages" and it will show you the most linked page on that URL.

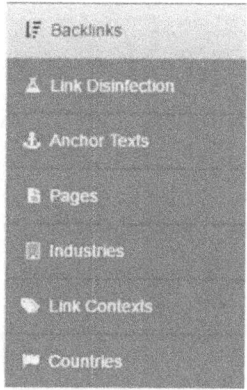

Use Buzzsumo to find heavily shared content in a specific topic. Just search for your keywords and set the search interval to at least one year.

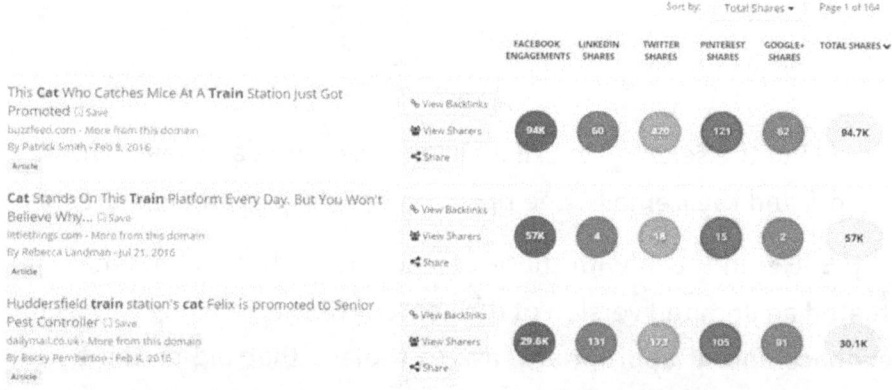

Step 2: Analyze the top content and make them much better. Sounds really easy, but trust me, it's damn hard. Here are some tips to get started: make it longer and more detailed, make it more up-to-date, use more visuals, and improve the design. You need to create epic content that will wow your audience.

Step 3: Our intention is to create better content than our competitor's and squeeze them out from the search ranking page. We need to find the people who linked to this content and convince them to link to your content instead.

You can use OpenLinkProfiler or Ahrefs to figure out who linked to any content. Enter the content's URL to see its backlinks. Filter the list according to domain authority so the highest ones will come first. Focus on only these.

US	Page title & link source	Anchor text & link destination	Index & cost	Added on
100%	Must-See New Tools for Small Business... ipage.com/blog/must-see-new-tools-for-small-businesses	Buffer buffer.com	computers blog	30 Sep 2016
100%	10 New Year's Resolutions to Improve ... ipage.com/blog/10-new-years-resolutions-to-improve-your-business	Buffer buffer.com	computers blog	30 Sep 2016
100%	Tips for Creating an Awesome Food Blog lifehack.org/470031/tips-for-creating-an-awesome-food-blog	Buffer buffer.com	computers blog	29 Sep 2016
100%	7 Essential Tools Every Serious Start... lifehack.org/465449/7-essential-tools-every-serious-startup-needs	Buffer buffer.com	computers standard	29 Sep 2016
100%	Top time-saving social media tools fo... godaddy.com/garage/webprofile/on/time-saving-social-media-tools	Pablo buffer.com/pablo	business standard	28 Sep 2016
100%	The Unsolicited UX Audit, Ep.1 – Deve... medium.com/developers-writing/the-unsolicited-ux-audit-ep-1 -105de8bb2c09	Buffer buffer.com	media standard	26 Sep 2016
100%	Buffer	crunchbase crunchbase.com/organization/buffer	http://buffer.com buffer.com · nofollow	business standard	22 Sep 2016
100%	The 12 Best Facebook Marketing Tools ... elegantthemes.com/blog/tips-tricks/best-facebook-marketing-tools- available-in-2016	Buffer buffer.com	media blog	18 Sep 2016

Step 4: Put the selected backlinks in an Excel sheet and search for the authors and their emails. See tip 11 on how to find email addresses.

Step 5: Get in touch with these people and let them know that you created an updated version of the content they are linking to. Ask for feedback and, if appropriate, ask to replace that old content with yours.

Tools:

Openlinkprofiler

Ahrefs

Buzzsumo

Recommended reading:

Link Building Case Study: How I Increased My Search Traffic by 110% in 14 Days

Viral Marketing Case Study: How a Brand New Blog Generated 17,584 Visitors In One Day

61. To the top!

Quite often we find blog posts with a title like: "The top content marketing blogs you need to follow" or "The best nutrition blogs you should read in 2016". There are tons of articles like this in almost every niche.

A few years ago I was dreaming about getting featured on list posts like these. I was wondering how the heck I could be discovered so these people will automatically include my blog in their list.

But the worst thing you can do is to wait to be discovered by someone, because the hard truth is that no one will. Especially if you have a small blog.

The best thing you can do is to escape from your cave and show yourself to these people.

Step 1: You need to find these list posts in your niche. I prepared some Google queries you can try:

Keyword + "top 10 sites"/"top sites"

Keyword + "top 10 websites"/"top websites"

Keyword + "useful sites"/"interesting sites"

Keyword + "favorite sites"

Keyword + "recommended websites"/"suggested websites"

Keyword + "useful websites"/"interesting websites"

Keyword + "favorite websites"

Keyword + "top blogs"

Keyword + "recommended blogs"

Step 2: Show your blog's value with a well-crafted pitch and attach some articles that you're the most proud of. Check tip 11 for finding the author's contact details.

Step 3: Get in touch with them via email and let them know that you exist and why your blog would be a good fit for their post. In some cases, the authors can't edit the post they have already published so just suggest your blog as a possible candidate for their next list post.

Recommended reading:

10000 Search Engine Queries for your Link Building Campaign

62. Resource pages

A form of content curation is to create a resource page for a given niche. Many bloggers pursue to create the best resource page for their given niche. They do it for the organic traffic and the social media shares coming from the authors of the featured articles.

This is also your opportunity to get your content featured on these resource pages. If your blog post is included then you will get a link back to your website, improving your domain authority and driving some referral traffic to that blog post.

This tactic is pretty similar to roundup posts, the only difference is that roundup posts are timely collections of blog posts (week's top blog posts, monthly roundup, etc.) while resource pages are collections of evergreen content.

Step 1: How to find resource pages in your niche? We need to use some Google queries to uncover these resource pages:

Keyword + "top resources"/"top resources"

Keyword + "top sites/"top sites"

Keyword + "top websites"/"top websites"

Keyword + "top articles"/ "top articles"

Keyword + "top web resources"/"top web resources"

Keyword + "top internet resources"/"top internet resources"

Keyword + "top online resources"/"top online resources"

Keyword + "recommended resources"/"suggested resources"

Keyword + "useful resources"/"interesting resources"

To see more queries visit this site.

Step 2: Create a list of these relevant resource pages. Include the authors' names and research their email addresses (see tip 11 how to do it).

Step 3: Share these resource pages on social media and add meaningful content to them. After engaging with the content, it's time to get in touch with the authors and ask their feedback on your content. If they really like it then they will include it automatically, otherwise, kindly ask for an inclusion. For more details on how to create successful outreach campaigns see tip 10.

Tools:

Contentmarketer.io

Recommended reading:

10000 Search Engine Queries for your Link Building Campaign

The anatomy of an insanely useful resource page

63. Find interview opportunities

I'm sure you've already seen blog posts that feature experts' answers regarding a specific question. Imagine that you're also featured on that list. In exchange for your answer, they will link back to your blog strengthening your domain authority and driving some referral traffic to your blog. How awesome would that be?

The good news is that you need only two things to nail it: you have to prove that you're an expert in your field and you need to be a bit proactive.

Step 1: You need to find blogs and bloggers that have already been featured in expert roundups. The best way to do it is by searching for it on Google. Here are some queries you could try:

industryName + intitle:interview

industryVertical + intitle:interview

competitorName + intitle:interview

industryName + inurl:interview

industryVertical + intitle:interview

competitorName + inurl:interview

Keyword + intitle:"experts interview"/talk/discuss/answer

Step 2: Put the article titles, links and author names in an Excel sheet for easier administration. All we need to do here is find their email addresses. Check out tip 11 for some sneaky tips.

Step 3: For better results, I highly recommend you build relationships with them first. If you need some tips on how to do it check out tip 10.

Here you can do two things:

141

First, write your own answer for that roundup post. In this case, the author just needs to paste your answers and do some formatting tasks. It takes just a few minutes and their article just got updated, which is good for SEO purposes. Even if they aren't able to edit that post they might consider you at their next expert roundup.

Second, simply ask the author to consider you in their next expert roundup. Don't forget to include some reference work and anything that proves you know what you're doing in your field.

Recommended reading:

How to Get Interviewed by Popular Blogs (Even If You're Not a Big Shot)

How to Land Big Interviews When Your Blog is Still Small

How to Get Interviewed 200 Times a year For Your Blog

64. Parasite SEO

Trust me, we aren't going to do anything illegal.

This tactic is especially useful when you're just starting out with a low authority site, because it would take your site much longer to rank for a competitive keyword. A high authority site will rank much faster than you.

We're going to capitalize on high authority websites to rank for a competitive keyword and drive traffic to your blog.

Step 1: Identify the keywords related to your niche and select the competitive ones you want to rank for. To check keyword competition, use Keyword Planner.

Step 2: Find relevant, high authority sites that partly or completely cover your niche. In Google search, the first 10 results probably belong to high authority sites. To check their domain authority score use this tool.

Step 3: Craft some content ideas (focusing on competitive keywords) and get in touch with the editors or the person who's responsible for guest contributions. Ask them if they're interested in your content ideas.

Step 4: If they're interested, write your guest post for that website. Make sure to include a relevant link in the body of your content that points back to your blog. They won't accept it if you just attach a random link from your website, it has to provide value to their readers.

Step 5: When writing that guest post, make sure that it's well optimized for that keyword. If it will rank well in search results then it will receive more organic traffic and so will your content you're linking to. For some optimization tips check out tip 65.

Tools:

Keyword Planner

Domain authority checker

Recommended reading:

7 Crucial Tactics for Writing a Wildly Successful Guest Post

The Ultimate Guide to Guest Blogging

The Definitive Guide to Guest Blogging

65. Organic traffic boost with onsite SEO

Onsite SEO refers to a set of web page optimization best practices that can be applied on your website to improve its ranking in search engine results.

The good thing is that the optimization is absolutely in your hands, you only need to follow the latest best practices to make your content well-optimized. However, onsite SEO is only part of the ranking factors, it's worth having a closer look to get the most out of your content.

You have to create the best content for that niche topic. In order to do that you, not only do you have to provide incredible value to your readers, but also have to pay attention to onsite SEO best practices.

Title tag: The title tag is a webpage's second most important onsite ranking factor. Make sure to include your focus keyword in the beginning of the title.

Heading in (h1): h1 tags are the second title tags of your content and send strong signals to Google. If appropriate, try to include your focus keyword in your h1 tags.

You can set a title as an h1 tag by using the Heading 1 formatting or in the source view of your content editor, simply put that title between the <h1> and <h1/> tags.

Link: Your links should be short, concise, and easily readable. Shorter URLs with fewer folders ("/" in the URL) tend to rank better.

Meta description: It serves as a description of your content. Include your focus keyword and other related keywords that support and describe your content

Content length: Longer content is preferred over shorter content since it can cover a topic in greater detail. Data shows that content around 2400 words ranks the best on Google.

Keywords: If your keyword appears a few times in your content, that sends a relevancy signal to Google, but avoid stuffing your content with keywords and only mention them 3-5 times.

Images: Embedded images in your content serve as important relevancy factors. Pay attention to your image's title, file name, caption, description and alt text.

Internal linking: Make sure to link not only to external sources but also to your own blog posts as well. Try to include these internal links as early as possible in your article. Not only does it make it much easier for your visitors to navigate around your site, but it also ensures that your site gets properly crawled, allowing the search engines to find all of your pages.

Tools:

Yoast SEO Wordpress (plugin)

SEO Site Checkup

Recommended reading:

Google's 200 Ranking Factors: The Complete List

On Page SEO – Everything You Need to Know

SEO 101: On-Page SEO Basics

66. Wikipedia link building hack

Wikipedia is one of the biggest and most authoritative websites on the internet. It's a link building golden mine. Wikipedia articles show up for almost every term and a link back to your website means a referral traffic boost to your blog.

There are two ways you can get backlinks from Wikipedia:

- Finding dead links

- Finding broken links

Step 1: Wikipedia actually has a dedicated page listing every article with a dead link. It could be a good starting point.

Or use this Google query for a more targeted search: site:wikipedia.org "Your keyword" "dead link"

Step 2: Visit one of the articles from the search results. On the page press Ctrl+F or Command+F and search for "dead link" to highlight the dead links.

Step 3: Copy the link and paste it to Way Back Time Machine to see what the page looked like. Read the content to make sure it's related to your website.

Step 4: Create original, up-to-date content that provides at least the same value and can replace the old one.

Step 5: Register or log in to Wikipedia. To fly under the radar, you should edit some other articles on Wikipedia for a few days. Fix grammar, make explanations simpler, add relevant images or update outdated information.

Step 6: Get back to your target article and replace the dead link with yours. Don't forget to add a note about the changes you've made, and then hit "Save page."

Pro tip: Don't overdo link building on Wikipedia. If you add lots of links, your website could be added to a spam list.

Tools:

Way Back Time Machine

Recommended reading:

Wikipedia Link Building Hack – Get As Many Backlinks As You Want

How Do I Use Wikipedia for SEO Purposes?

How Small Businesses Can Get a Link from Wikipedia

67. Traffic boost from old posts

You can bring your old posts back to life by updating, upgrading and repurposing them.

It's an efficient way to save some time but still give value to your readers and also good for boosting the organic traffic of these posts.

Brian Dean used this tactic at his blog and he was able to increase the organic traffic of one blog post by 111.37%. I also tried his tip and I experienced a 60-70 percent organic traffic increase for the updated posts.

Step 1: Your blog posts shouldn't be treated equally. Only select the posts that had the biggest positive impact on your business. Check out in Google analytics how your posts performed, just navigate to "Behavior" and select "Overview".

Step 2: Here are some metrics you should pay attention to:

- Goal conversion rates

- Time on page

- Bounce rate

- Social shares (use this bulk social share checker)

- Backlinks (use this backlink checker)

Step 3: According to your data, prioritize your posts and start with the most important ones. Here are some tips on updating your post. The more you change, the bigger the impact will be.

- Adding new tips

- Updating information

- Including new images

- Making it more detailed

For more tips on improving on site SEO see tip 65.

Tools:

Bulk Social Checker

Bulk Backlink Checker

Recommended reading:

21 Actionable SEO Techniques You Can Use Right Now (Updated)

How to Update Old Posts On Your Blog (and When You Should Consider Doing it)

Why and How to Properly Update Old Blog Posts

68. Smart guest blogging

Writing guest posts should be part of every content marketing strategy. Creating content for authority sites can increase your brand awareness, increases your website's authority and you can get some referral traffic from these websites.

To make your guest blogging effort more efficient, you need to make this process more focused and need to make the necessary preparations.

Step 1: Find websites your target audience frequently visits. If you know at least one website, you can find many similar ones by simply doing a Google search. Just use this query: related: "www.example.com".

It will show you every site that's considered similar to your target website. Check them one by one and make sure they accept guest contributions. Here you can find a list of websites that accept guest contributions.

Step 2: Once you have a list of potential websites, check their domain authority score with this bulk checker tool. Start focusing on only the ones with the highest authority. These websites provide the biggest return on your efforts.

Step 3: Before you start bombarding them with your content ideas, create some really awesome content. This is quite useful for two reasons: First, it serves as a reference and increases your chances of your approval. Second, you will link back to this content from your guest content.

Step 4: Generate content ideas that could be a good fit for your target sites, include your references and reach out to them. Once you get approved and the guest content is selected, make sure to find a way to appropriately include a link back to your website. They usually allow you to add one link back to your website, but this link has to provide real value to the readers. Otherwise, it will be removed by the editor.

Tools:

Bulk Domain Authority Checker

Recommended reading:

How to Generate Meaningful Content Ideas

How to Write a Guest Post Pitch That Gets Accepted Every Time

How to Find Guest Blogging Opportunities (+189 Email Addresses to Pitch)

Part 6: Communities & Directories

Learn how to use content directories and other platforms as part of your content marketing strategy. This section will provide some tips on how to use new and old platforms to reach your target audience.

69. Content directories

Directories categorize your blog based on its content. You can get extra traffic from these directories since your blog can be found in many relevant sub categories. They also provide links to your blog (some of them do follow backlinks) so it can boost your ranking in search engines.

You're lucky! I already did the heavy lifting for you. If you want to save time, here is a list of 100+ directories with domain authority scores. Click here to download it for free.

You can also check out the recommended reading section for at least a hundred different blog directories. Also, here is a tool that automatically submits your blog to multiple directories.

Step 1: Check out the websites and create your own list in an Excel sheet.

Step 2: Make sure that submitting your blog to that directory is worth your time by checking their domain authority score. You can use Seoweather or Checkmoz for that.

Step 3: Sort this list according to domain authority and register at the higher domain authority sites first.

Tools:

Seoweather

153

Checkmoz

Seoreviewtools

Recommended reading:

10 Blog Directories Actually Worth Your Time

131+ Manually Verified Free Blog Directories To Submit Your Blog

RSS – Blog Directories

70. Get traffic from content curation sites

There are thousands of people out there collecting and sharing great stuff with others. There are dedicated websites for content curation where you can find these people and even suggest your content for curation.

Most of them don't provide do-follow links that would boost your search ranking, but they do provide links to your blog and content so you can get some traffic from these websites.

In this case, we're focusing on the most popular one: Scoop.it.

Step 1: Register a free account at Scoop.it and search for the keyword variations that best describe your freshly published content.

Step 2: Make sure to focus on only relevant boards with a high number of frequent visitors. Create a separated list in an Excel file so they can be easily managed.

Step 3: Start suggesting your new content to the curator of these collections. If suggestion is not allowed on their board then get in touch with them on social media or via email.

Tools:

Collexio

Paperli

Scoop.it

List.ly

Recommended reading:

50 killer tools for discovering, sharing, and scheduling the best content

155

7 top tools for content curation

5 smart tricks to drive more website traffic with content curation

How Content Curation Can Drive Traffic

71. Double social sharing with one button

If your readers prefer to use Slack, it's worth considering **adding an "Add to Slack" button to your emails**. This is what Aladdin Happy did in his Growth Hacking newsletter, successfully doubling his social shares.

Step 1: Go to AddThis.com and register a free account. Here is a code you should insert to your email newsletter after customization:

*https://dashboard.addthis.com/darkseid/slack-oauth/auth?shareURL=**INPUT_HERE_YOUR_ENCODED_URL%23.V2 PAktNb29I.slack**&shareTitle=**INPUT_HERE_YOUR_ENCODED_TEXT***

Note: Only modify the INPUT_HERE_YOUR_ENCODED_URL and the INPUT_HERE_YOUR_ENCODED_TEXT in the code.

Step 3: Copy your blog post's link you would like to be shared and go to URL Encoder to get the encoded URL. Paste your link and click encode.

Step 4: Copy the message that you want to be shared to generate the encoded text. Paste your message and click encode.

Step 5: Replace the bold parts of the code with your encoded URL and text. Copy the code and insert to your newsletter. This is what it should look like:

Tools:

AddThis

Text and URL encoder

Recommended reading:

Slacklist

72. Promote content in Slack groups

In the last few years, Slack rapidly emerged from nothing, gaining millions of users in a really short period of time. Now, Slack is one of the most used tools for team communication and communities.

Slack isn't just a platform where you can randomly throw your content and expect huge traffic. This isn't how it works. There are communities on Slack covering many different areas. Your goal must be to join these communities and provide as much value as you can: give feedback, ask questions, and help others.

Most of these groups won't allow you to promote your own stuff. Even if you can't use a Slack community to directly promote your content, you can get in touch with your target audience or fellow marketers who might help you later in your content marketing efforts.

Step 1: Find relevant Slack communities. You can simply do a search on Google to find a Slack community or just checkout the recommended reading for a list of communities.

Step 2: Request to join these communities. It could take a few days until you get accepted by an admin.

Step 3: Start engaging with your communities, introduce yourself and share an interesting story about yourself. Follow and start discussions.

Step 4: After you brought value to the community and members are allowed to share their own content, you can share yours and ask for feedback from the members.

Tools:

Slack

159

Slacklist

Recommended reading:

An Incomplete List of Communities on Slack

12 Best Slack Communities for Every Professional

73. Product Hunt isn't just for products

Product Hunt used to be a community where product enthusiasts can share and up vote the latest cool products they have found. Now, Product Hunt is much more. It's not just a community for product people, but also a community for games, books, podcasts and many more. Submitting your newest guide/giveaway to the book section is a great way to give it a further boost and generate more leads.

Step 1: To maintain a healthy volume of submissions each day, only a limited number of people have access to comment and post on Product Hunt. So without receiving an invitation, you won't be able to post on Product Hunt, but you can register and up vote other submissions. I recommend you sign up with your Twitter account so your followers who are also registered on the platform will also be your followers there.

Step 2: Product Hunt is a community so you should start making friends there. Get in touch with people who have already submitted books related to your field. Ask their feedback on your giveaway and if they like it, you can ask them to submit it to Product Hunt or later you can ask for an invitation so you can do it yourself.

Tools:

Product Hunt

Recommended reading:

7 tips for Product Hunt success

Product Hunt: The Comprehensive Guide to Getting Featured

How I Got Featured on Product Hunt And What Happened Next

74. Forums are still alive!

I read somewhere that promoting your content on online forums actually can drive some extra traffic to your content. Some of them receive millions of visitors each month. Honestly, I was really surprised. I didn't even know that forums are still used and wasn't sure of their ability to drive traffic to your blog.

You have to start using them to decide if it's something worth adding to your content promotion strategy or not. Follow the steps below to figure it out for yourself.

Step 1: First we need to find forums that are related to your field. A simple way to do it is by using this Google query: "niche +forum" or this one: "intitle:forum" + niche keyword

(make sure to replace "niche" with keywords that describes your blog). You can also check this Wikipedia page for an incomplete list.

Step 2: After a certain number of forums, it will be difficult to track where you're registered. I recommend you create a list of forums in an Excel sheet or just simply bookmark them in your browser.

Step 3: Register at these forums and start engaging in the community. When you see a great opportunity to share your own content, do it by including more than one source. It makes you less suspicious since you share a variety of resources. This camouflage is strongly recommended since forums usually have really strict rules. Sometimes it's not even permitted to post a link in your comment.

Pro tip: When registering on a forum, don't use your blog's email address and your real identity. The thing is that some forums are quite sensitive when someone shares her own content. Even if it helps to solve an issue, you can get easily banned for it. This is why I had to say goodbye to one of the biggest online marketing forums.

Recommended reading:

[Blog Traffic Tips Weekly Newsletter](#)

[5 Secrets to Promote Your Site Via Forum](#)

75. Quora Hack

Quora is a question-and-answer website where questions are asked, answered, edited and organized by its community of users. You can drive targeted traffic from Quora to your content by leaving answers on relevant questions. It works like an information market; there are people with questions and there are other users who can answer those questions. This is a place where information demand and supply meet.

But instead of answering relevant questions randomly, in this case we will follow a more focused approach by Matthew Barby.

Step 1: Go to SEMrush.com. SEMrush is a competitive intelligence suite for online marketing, from SEO and PPC to social media and video advertising research.

Step 2: Enter "quora.com" to the label in the middle of the screen and hit enter. From the left menu, under the "Domain Analytics" section, click on "Organic Research".

Step 3: It will list the top ranking questions on Quora. Run a search for a keyword related to your content (you need to login to do that). Sort the results in descending order by search volume.

Step 4: Start high! Add your answer to the question with the highest search volume.

For more Q&A sites like Quora, check out this exhaustive list.

Tools:

SEMrush

Recommended reading:

How We Answer Quora Questions to Drive Traffic to Our Website

How to Turn Quora into a Traffic-Driving Machine for Your Blog

76. Content communities

There are many niche communities specialized in different topics, such as films, gaming, programming, marketing, etc. These communities don't just bring people with common interests together, but also let members submit the latest, coolest content.

The success of each submitted content lies in the power of the community. Members can up vote the content others submitted and the most voted (popular) submission will receive the highest exposure on the platform, meaning more traffic to that content.

These communities could be your traffic golden mine, but it takes time and effort to achieve that since most of these communities demand interaction from their members.

Step 1: Find relevant communities in your field. Check out the recommended reading for a bunch of communities or simply do some Google searches to find them. I created a list to get you started; you can download it from here.

Step 2: I know it's quite tempting to share your content right after the registration but please don't do that. Even if it generates some traffic, in the long term, it's not a sustainable solution. We're not here for the quick wins.

Instead, engage with others in the communities by up voting their submissions, leaving comments, asking and answering questions.

Pro tip: You can even directly contact some members from the community. I did it one by one until I got in touch with 40 people from the same community. It was easy to contact them since we're in the same community (have something in common) and also gave some feedback on their content they submitted (another mutual point). In 90% of the cases, we had really great conversations and I always let them know that I'm ready to help their submissions with an up vote and feedback. I gave them what I wanted to receive in the long run, engagement and up votes from community members. Surprisingly, around 50% of them offered the same help for me. Bingo.

Step 3: When I have great content to submit to the community, I always get in touch with my closest friends from that community. I simply want to get some feedback on my content and if they like my stuff then I ask them to submit it to the community or help my submission with an up vote or comment.

Tools:

Nimble

Recommended reading:

How to Build Relationships through Communities

Part 7: Repurposing Content

Your content can be transformed into many different formats. Tips from this chapter will reveal how to use infographics, ebooks, email courses and other content formats to increase your website traffic and generate more leads.

77. Apple News

Apple News is a pre-installed application on every iOS device (version iOS 9 or later). The app delivers traditional text-based content, videos, and photo galleries from a variety of sources, including magazines, websites, and newspapers.

By syndicating your content on Apple News, you could get extra exposure for your content. Once you publish an article, it's added to the Apple News app, and the content is automatically optimized for all iOS devices.

Step 1: Sign <u>into your iCloud account</u> with your Apple ID (which is your device's associated ID).

Step 2: Fill out your publisher information and provide additional information to set up your channel.

Step 3: You can choose from two different publishing methods: RSS feed (there's no change in user experience, which means you can't use Apple's article format) or the Apple News Format, which optimizes your content for iOS devices.

Step 4: After you're approved as a publisher, you're required to submit some articles for review. To do that, you can either create an article in News Publisher or use your existing content management system (CMS).

To create an article in News Publisher, sign in and select News Publisher from the menu. If you need further information about the features, check out the official guide.

If you prefer to connect your CMS with News Publisher, you'll need to use a plugin or write the code yourself. Here are plugins for WordPress and Drupal:

- Publish to Apple News (Wordpress plugin)
- Publish to Apple News (Drupal plugin)

In each case, Apple reviews your articles and notifies you as soon as your content is approved. After that, you can publish without further review.

Tools:

Wordpress: Publish to Apple News

Drupal: Publish to Apple News

Recommended Reading:

How to Publish Content on Apple News: A Step-by-Step Guide

How to publish on the new iOS 9 Apple 'News' app

How to Connect Your WordPress Powered Site to Apple News Publisher

78. Infographics

Infographics are candies for our brains. They're engaging, catch our attention and make information consuming faster. In fact, infographics are liked and shared 3x more on social media than any other type of content.

Eye-tracking studies revealed that readers spend more time looking at information-carrying images if they're relevant.

Visual content shared on Pinterest has a longer lifecycle compared to other content formats. Pins receive 40 percent of all the clicks within the first day and 70 percent take place in the first two days, the last 30 percent of clicks within the course of a month.

Infographics receive more engagement on social media, have a longer lifecycle online and people spend more time looking at them than at text. Sounds like a golden mine; all we need to do is to start crafting infographics, right?

Step 1: You don't necessary have to start from scratch. Your old blog posts are great sources and make the process a bit faster since you don't have to collect all the data. Check out your popular blog posts and see if you can transform them into an infographic.

Step 2: The only problem is that creating infographics takes a hell of a lot of time, but as you can see, the data above makes it worth the effort. If you're not a Photoshop ninja, welcome to the club. There are some great tools out there that make it super easy to create really nice infographics. See the tool suggestions below.

Step 3: Once you're done, send it out to bloggers whose audience might find it useful. If they like it then they will probably use it in their next post or simply share it with their followers.

Step 4: You can also submit it to websites dedicated to infographics. Here is a list of websites:

- Visual.ly

- Daily Infographic

- Cool Infographics

- Infographics Archive

- Infographic Journal

- Visual Loop

- Pinterest

If you're hungry for more, here is an insane list of one hundred infographic directories:

Tools:

Piktochart

Canva

Venngage

Recommended reading:

9 Ways to Improve Your Pinterest Marketing

5 Pinterest Strategies That Drive Big Traffic

4 Ways to Optimize Pinterest Content for Engagement and SEO

79. Directories for your content giveaways

I know it sounds weird. You are offering this giveaway in exchange for an email address. This is an incentive for your readers to convert and we're giving it for free without asking for their contact details.

With this guide, our intention is to get people to visit your blog and offer them another giveaway for download.

Implementing this tip could result in more traffic and new subscribers for your blog.

Step 1: Modify your original guide and make sure to include some call to actions pointing back to your blog. Everyone can download your guide without providing their email address so this is why it's important to add some calls to action.

Step 2: Upload your giveaway to Guides.co. For easier navigation, you may need to edit your guide. Here is a list of other websites where you can submit your guides.

Recommended reading:

Tim Paige Reveals How to Create the Perfect Lead Magnet

The 7 Characteristics of a Perfect Lead Magnet

5 Ways To Come Up With A Perfect Lead Magnet For Your Blog

80. Email courses from old posts

There are many ways to convince your readers to subscribe to your newsletter and become your frequent visitors. You can create downloadable guides, transform your blog posts into PDF documents, and offer checklists and similar content to convince them to opt-in.

But creating downloadable content is not the only way to incentivize visitors to convert. You can also create an email course for your readers. The good thing is you probably don't have to start from scratch. You only need to use your old blog posts.

Step 1: Based on your already published content, what could be the focus of your email course that actually delivers value to your readers? Here is an example: Do you teach people how to play golf? Convert your current content into a 30-day course: Learn to play golf in 30 days.

Step 2: Slice up these articles and make sure each piece provides value to your subscribers. You should transform each piece of a tip into a standalone email.

Step 3: Add these emails to your email automation software, such as Getresponse or Mailchimp. In Mailchimp, you can create different lists so you can easily segment your subscriber base. Create a separate list for people who took your email course.

Step 4: Under the "Automation" menu, search for "Welcome message" and click "Add automation".

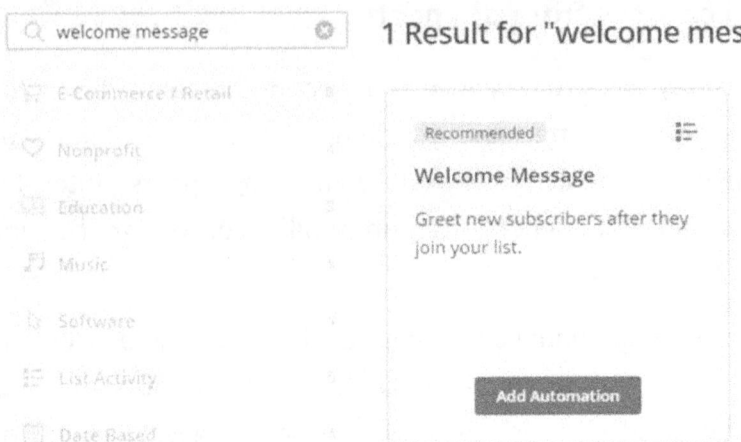

Give it a name and connect it to the previously created list. Note: you need to have a paid account to do that.

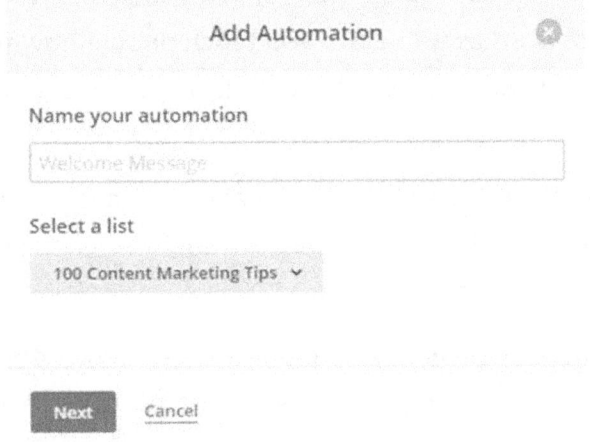

Step 5: Customize its settings and don't forget to set the trigger event to "Immediately after subscribers join your list". Add your tips to the first email and schedule others for automated sending. I recommend you leave seven days between each email.

Step 6: Create a call to action on your website, promoting your email course. It could be an embedded CTA on your blog posts, a bar on top of your website or a popup pointing to a landing page with an opt-in form.

Tools:

Mailchimp

Getresponse

Hellobar

SumoMe

Recommended reading:

5 Best Practices for Creating an Email Course

How to Create an Email Course that Rocks

17 Tips & Best Practices for Writing Catchy Email Subject Lines

81. Transform your content into a presentation

Did you know that Slideshare is also a search engine for presentations? This website is the home of professional content visited by more than 70 million people each month.

Repurposing your content is not just a way to offer your blog post in a different format, but also a great way to rank it on a different search engine like Slideshare.

To transform your content into a presentation, you can use Powerpoint or Keynote, but you can also try other cool tools, like Haikudeck or Prezi.

Your already published posts serve as a good foundation for your new presentation. Here are some tips on how to create amazing presentations that will generate traffic to your blog:

Tip 1: Use your content's headline as your Slideshare title and the subheadings as transition slides.

Tip 2: Link back to your website multiple times within your presentation so slide viewers can dig deeper if they want. These links could be related articles, a landing page or the original post.

Make sure to add UTM parameters to the links so you can accurately measure the performance of each link. Use this UTM parameter generator or learn more about it here.

Tip 3: Create a stylish design for your presentation. It's recommended to use only two colors (a light and a dark one). Here is a free tool for generating color schemes.

Tip 4: If you use images in your presentation, make sure to use high-quality, royalty free images. Check out tip 9 for a list of websites with free, high-quality images.

177

Tip 5: Fonts actually matter, so don't forget to find the perfect font combination for your slides. If you need help, try this free tool.

Tip 6: When uploading your presentation to Slideshare, include your target keywords in the title, build curiosity with your description and add related tags.

Tip 7: The best time to upload your Slideshare is 2am (EST). This timing gives your presentation the highest chance to make it on the first page.

Tip 8: Don't forget to embed your presentation in your original post. On Slideshare, under your presentation, click the "Share" button, copy and insert the code to your website.

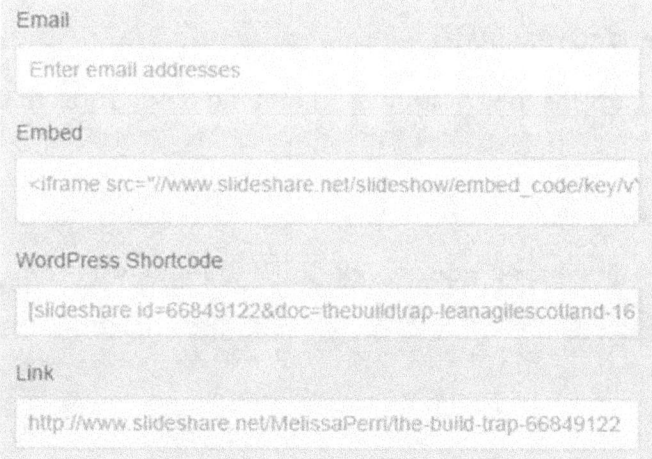

Other websites to submit your presentation:

- Scribd
- SlideRocket
- Authorstream
- Slideboom
- My Brainshark

- PowerShow
- Slideserve

Tools:

Power Point

Haikudeck

Prezi

Colors

Canva Font Combinations

Campaign URL Builder

Recommended reading:

How to Get Insane Amounts of Traffic and Subscribers from SlideShare

Slideshare Traffic Case Study

Breaking SlideShare: How I Got 2,000,000 Views from Only 16 Presentations

82. Your e-book on Amazon

Amazon.com is a huge search engine. Among many different products, millions of people are searching for books. This is your opportunity to repurpose your content into an e-book and publish it on amazon.com.

Our goal with this tactic is to generate extra traffic and new leads for your blog by giving away content for free.

Your e-book has to provide value to your readers and has to meet Amazon's strict regulations.

Step 1: Do a keyword search on your keyword that is related to your content. Try different variations and other close keywords. Our intention is to see how many people are searching for your potential keywords. Use this free tool to see the Amazon queries with volume.

I recommend you list your potential keywords in an Excel sheet and type the search volume next to them. Prioritize the keywords according to volume.

Step 2: Select your focus keywords that will be included in your book's title. Amazon allows you to add seven additional keywords to your book, select the ones with the highest volume.

Step 3: Make your guide compatible with Kindle. I recommend you do it manually or hire someone, since most of the automatic tools aren't that accurate. Here is a guide you should follow.

Pro tip: Make sure to funnel as many readers as possible to your blog. Here are some ways you can do it:

- Link back to your blog posts

- Inert calls to action (buttons, banners, texts) to your book

- Create a dedicated page for bonus content (place one near the beginning, one in the middle and another one closer to the end)

Step 4: Log in or register here and upload your book in <u>Kindle format</u>.

Some areas you have to pay attention to:

- Select the appropriate categories (max 2) for your book

- Create a book cover that stands out from these categories (Canva)

- Make sure your title contains your main keyword

- Add other related keywords with high search volume (max 7)

- Write a detailed description (like a blog post), use HTML formatting to highlight sections (here is an <u>HTML generator</u>)

- Set the price for free

Done? Preview your book and if everything looks great, go to the next step.

Step 5: Publish and start promoting your post. Your goal is to generate as many downloads and good reviews as possible. The number of downloads (sales) and the quality of reviews highly determines the ranking of your book. Some tips on promotion:

- Notify your subscribers

- Ask friends to download and review

- Try free Kindle groups on Facebook

- Submit to free Kindle promo sites. See list in the recommended reading.

Tools:

Merchantwords

Canva

HTML Generator

Recommended reading:

79 Free Book Promotion Sites To Advertise Your Ebook On

Kindle Launch Plan: Publish and Market an Amazon Bestseller

How Book Marketing Really Works: Tips from a 6-Figure Self-Published Author

83. Out of the box: grader

Content marketing is about giving value to your target audience and building long lasting relationships with them. Now, just try to think outside of the box. You can use anything that helps your target audience and builds connections with them.

It doesn't have to be a blog post, a webinar, a podcast or an infographic. It could be something else, such as an online grader.

Hubspot's website grader was a simple form and when a website link and email address was submitted, someone from the Hubspot team manually analyzed and sent the results back to the given email address. It scores many aspects of your online marketing, such as social media, blogging, SEO and website performance.

After a certain amount of submissions, automation was necessary and now it's an award winning online tool that graded 4 million websites.

Just think about your audience and the way you can help them. Could you create your own grader that gives them value?

As you see in the example above, it doesn't have to be a real, fully automated tool at first. It can be easily managed manually in an early phase.

Creating a grader could be efficient to generate more traffic and leads for your blog. For inspiration, see the recommended reading section.

Recommended reading:

7 Indispensable (and Free!) Website Graders and Content Scores

13 free website and marketing grader tools

Part 8: Conversion

This chapter will help you find new ways to generate more leads and some hacks on how to improve the conversion rates of your opt-in forms.

84. Capture emails directly from Twitter

Imagine a situation when you could place your signup forms on your Twitter timeline. Your followers could easily download your e-book directly from Twitter and you could get their email addresses. Good news, this is real. You can do it on Twitter by using Twitter's Lead Generation Cards.

People won't visit your website to download your e-book, but they will download it and in exchange they will give you their email addresses. Following this tip you will be able to capture some extra leads from Twitter and add them to your mailing list to keep them regularly visiting your website.

Step 1: You need to sign up for Twitter's ad platform to use Lead Generation Cards. To activate your ad account, you need to add your credit card information, but keep calm, you won't spend anything on Twitter.

Step 2: Register at Tweetlead.io and under the "Tweet Card URLs" menu, add a new URL. Make sure you connect it to your newsletter tool.

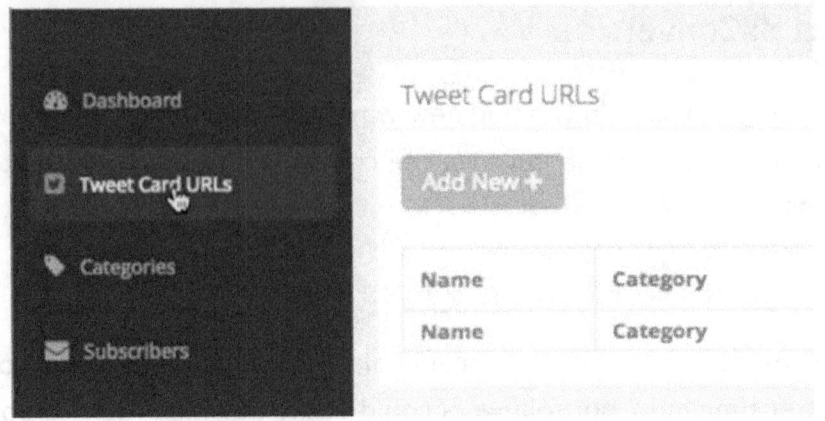

If it's done, a new URL will appear on your dashboard. Copy it to the clipboard and go to the next step.

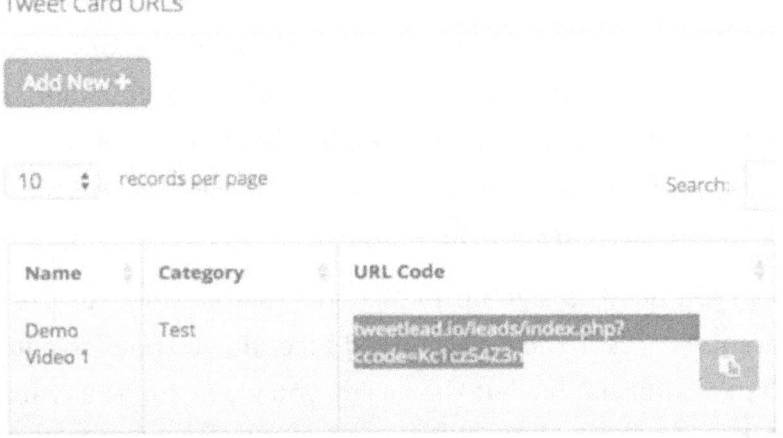

Step 3: Go back to your Twitter ads account and from the upper menu, select "Creatives" and create your Twitter Card.

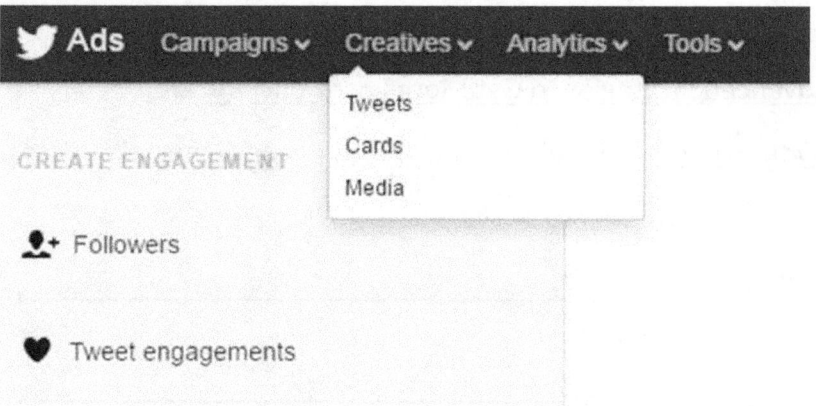

Important: Under the "Data section", paste the URL you previously copied. This is where the submitted data will be passed.

▾ Data settings (optional)

If you choose not to specify these settings, you can always downl

Please complete the following technical settings in order for Twitte Generation card. We recommend you read the Lead Generation (

Submit URL ⓐ

| https:// | |

Information below will be sent to your Submit URL.

You can provide custom key names and custom hidden fields that data.

Note: If you don't connect your Twitter card with Tweetlead.io then you have to manually copy your leads from Twitter to your own mailing system. That's not fun.

Tools:

Tweetlead.io

Recommended reading:

Create your Lead Card

How to Use Twitter for Lead Generation

6 Advanced Strategies to Get More Leads on Twitter

How to Grow Your Email List with Twitter Lead Generation Cards

85. Double subscribing rate with targeted popups

I have been experimenting with pop ups a lot. So far for me, exit intent pop ups worked the best, but you can also make them appear while your visitor is reading your article or reaches a specific part of your content. No matter which option you choose, you need to pay attention to targeting. This is how we were able to double our form's conversion rate and acquired two times more subscribers.

Step 1: For creating targeted popups, you need to register a paid account at Hellobar.com.

Step 2: Click "Create new" from the menu and set the goal and customize your popup text and design.

Step 3: The magic trick comes at the targeting section. You can make this popup appear only on a given article. Let's say your reader visits an article about social media images, and then you can set up a unique popup just for that article, offering related downloadable

bonus content on social media images in exchange for their email address.

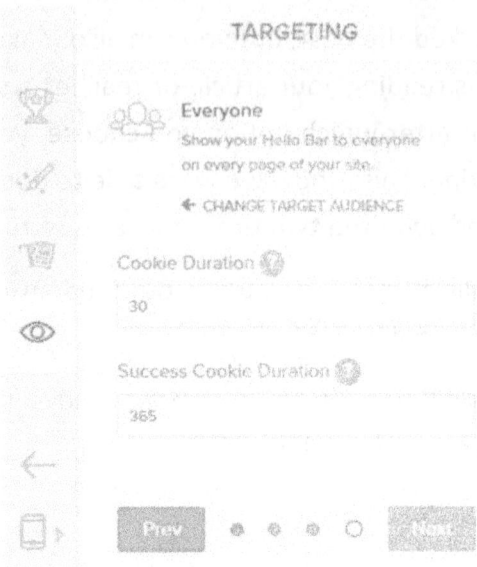

All you need to do is to create an audience segment for that article so the popup will be shown for those who are currently visiting that specific article. This way you can make sure you're offering relevant bonus content.

Tools:

Hellobar

Recommended reading:

How to Make Your Popups Irresistible (And Not Annoying)

6 Headline Formulas That Will Make Your Popup Irresistible to Read

8 Tips for Using Popups to Grow Your Mailing List (Without Annoying Your Visitors)

189

86. Turn your blog post into a lead magnet

One of the most important things you should focus on is building your email list. It's not just the most efficient way to keep in touch with your followers, it's also platform independent so you're not exposed to algorithm changes.

The hardest part is finding new ways to capture more and more emails on your website. I tried a rather long tail tactic that further boosted our lead generation efforts. With this tactic, we were able to get an extra 30-40 leads per post. I simply offered my blog post as a downloadable PDF. It was really effective compared to the effort I put into it.

Step 1: Add the "Print Friendly & PDF" extension to your blog.

Step 2: Once you published your post, go to the post's page and click on "Print Friendly & PDF" from your browser extensions or visit Printfriendly.com and submit your post's link.

Step 3: It will automatically generate a PDF version of your post. In the preview, you can make minor adjustments to make it look better. Save and upload it to your CMS.

Step 4: Create a banner that will be embedded in your blog post. You can use Canva or just a simple PPT template (see recommended reading). If you use the PDF templates, make sure to highlight every element of the CTA. Right click on the selected objects and Save as image.

Step 5: Insert it to your blog post as an image and make sure to attach a link to the banner that points to a landing page where your readers can access it.

Tools:

Canva

Powerpoint

Print Friendly & PDF

Recommended reading:

How To Create CTAs that Actually Cause Action

21 Call to Action Examples and 3 Rules for Effective CTAs

How to Easily Create Professional-Looking CTAs in PowerPoint [Tutorial]

87. Embedded calls to action

The sad truth is that our readers have a very limited attention span online. The introduction of your post is supposed to catch your readers, convincing them to stay longer and read your stuff.

But our intention here is not just to keep your visitor reading your post, but also to convert them into subscribers and keep them frequently coming back.

If they like your post then their attention will be focused on it, so a great way to put your CTAs in the spotlight is by embedding them in the body of your post.

It can be a simple call to action to subscribe to your newsletter, but there are more efficient ways to convert them by giving something in exchange for their email address. It could increase subscribe rates by 300-400%.

Step 1: You need to create an image that will be embedded in your blog post. You can use drag and drop image editors, like Canva or Powerpoint, to create a CTA in minutes.

Step 2: Insert that image to your blog post where appropriate. You can even embed it more than once. Don't forget to attach a link to that picture that points to your signup form or a landing page where they can access the content after submitting their email address.

Tools:

Canva

Powerpoint

Recommended reading:

10 techniques for an effective 'call to action'

17 Best Practices for Crazy-Effective Call-To-Action Buttons

How To Design Call to Action Buttons That Convert

88. Displaying popup on Page load

There are many ways you can experiment with popups on your website. One of my favorite bloggers, Robbie Richards ran a test and found that popups appearing right after the page loaded had 91.06% higher conversion rates than exit-intent popups.

Step 1: Register a free account or login at hellobar.com and click "Create New". If you haven't installed Hello Bar on your website, make sure to insert its code between the head section of your website.

Step 2: Select your campaign's goal and during the customization, set the popup type as modular or page takeover and make sure it will displayed immediately after the page loads.

Step 3: At the design and content step, you can upload a picture of the e-book. If you offer an e-book in exchange for an email, attaching an e-book image to the form could increase the conversion rate by 110.72%.

Tools:

Hellobar

SumoMe

Recommended reading:

Pop-ups Aren't Dead: What We Learned Analyzing 2 Billion Pop-up Examples

40 Top Brands Using Pop-Ups to Increase Their Conversions

6 Essential Tips to Boost Your Popup Conversions

89. Viral lead generation

An efficient way to get extra subscribers is through recommendations from friends. UpViral is a viral referral system that allows you to create viral giveaways that will get people to promote your website.

You can use this referral system when offering special content for download. When someone enters their email address, they will automatically get a unique invite link. This link will track how many people she refers.

Your visitors will get the special content if they refer enough people. This is a good incentive to get more leads for your content by creating a viral loop.

Step 1: First you need to create a new campaign and select your target. You can set up your own landing page (lead page) by UpViral or embed its code to your current one. UpViral offers pretty great integration, so it can save a lot of time if you choose an UpViral landing page.

Step 2: The 'Thank you' page plays a crucial part. On this page, you will convince your subscribers to share your content and they will also see their unique link and their progress. All you need to do is to customize your thank you page using UpViral's editor.

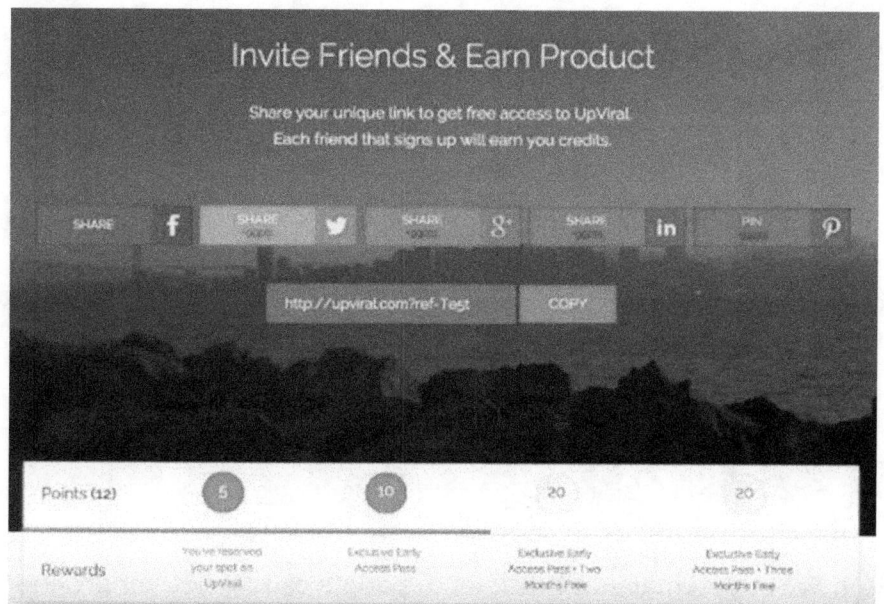

Step 3: Design the social appearance of your content so people will want to share it on social media. Make sure to create a catchy headline, attach a nice image and, if you prefer, add your Twitter handle as well. Leave some space (at least 10-15 characters) so they can easily edit and add further things to the post.

Step 4: Under the reward section, you can set up what people will get after sharing. They can get points for sharing your content on social media and also points after each new referred registered user. Here you can upload the content people will receive after inviting enough people.

Step 5: Set up email notifications so people can track their progress and get notified as soon as his content is unlocked. It's separate from your email autoresponder tool, managed by UpViral.

Step 6: Connect UpViral with your newsletter tool so you can capture those submitted emails. Fortunately, it's compatible with many services.

Tools:

UpViral

Mailchimp

Getresponse

Recommended reading:

Upviral Review and Case Study

Referral Program Examples – An Epic List Of 47 Referral Programs

The 39 Best Referral Program Examples of 2014

197

Part 9: Keep More People Coming Back

In this section, you will read tips on how to keep subscribers coming back by making your email marketing more efficient, using Facebook remarketing and other techniques to boost retention.

90. Boost newsletter open rates by 3-4%

Keeping your existing subscribers coming back is much easier than converting new visitors into subscribers. The best way to keep in touch with your subscribers is by sending them regular newsletters. It would be so awesome if everyone opened and clicked your newsletter. Unfortunately, it never happens. People are busy and receive a ton of emails every day. Even if they like you, chances are that some of your emails will be buried deep down in their mailbox. It's time to give them a second chance! You can increase open rates by re-sending your newsletter to those who haven't opened it yet.

Step 1: Send out your newsletter and make sure to wait at least 48 hours.

Step 2: Check out the analytics of your email campaign and separate those who haven't opened your newsletter. I like to paste them to an Excel sheet.

Step 3: Create a new campaign in your newsletter tool and add everyone who hasn't opened your email.

Step 4: Change the title of your original email and hit send again (see tip 6 for crafting catchy subject lines).

Tools:

Mailchimp

Getresponse

Recommended reading:

12 Powerful Tips to Dramatically Increase Email Open Rate

10 Easy Ways to Improve Your Email Open Rate

7 Simple Ways To Improve Your Email Open Rates

91. Keep readers coming back without social media and newsletter

There's no doubt that building a social media following and capturing emails for your newsletters are effective ways to keep your readers coming back. Browser push notifications are alternative ways to keep in touch with your readers, not the competitor of social media and email marketing.

By using push notifications for Chrome browser (and Firefox), you can still keep your readers coming back without asking for their email addresses.

Step 1: Register a free account on Pushcrew's website.

Step 2: You will get a unique code that should be inserted in the head section of your website. If you have a WordPress site, just install this plugin.

Step 3: You need to customize your push notification, since the default version is pretty weird. Fortunately, among many things, you can edit the title, subtitle and button text of your notification window.

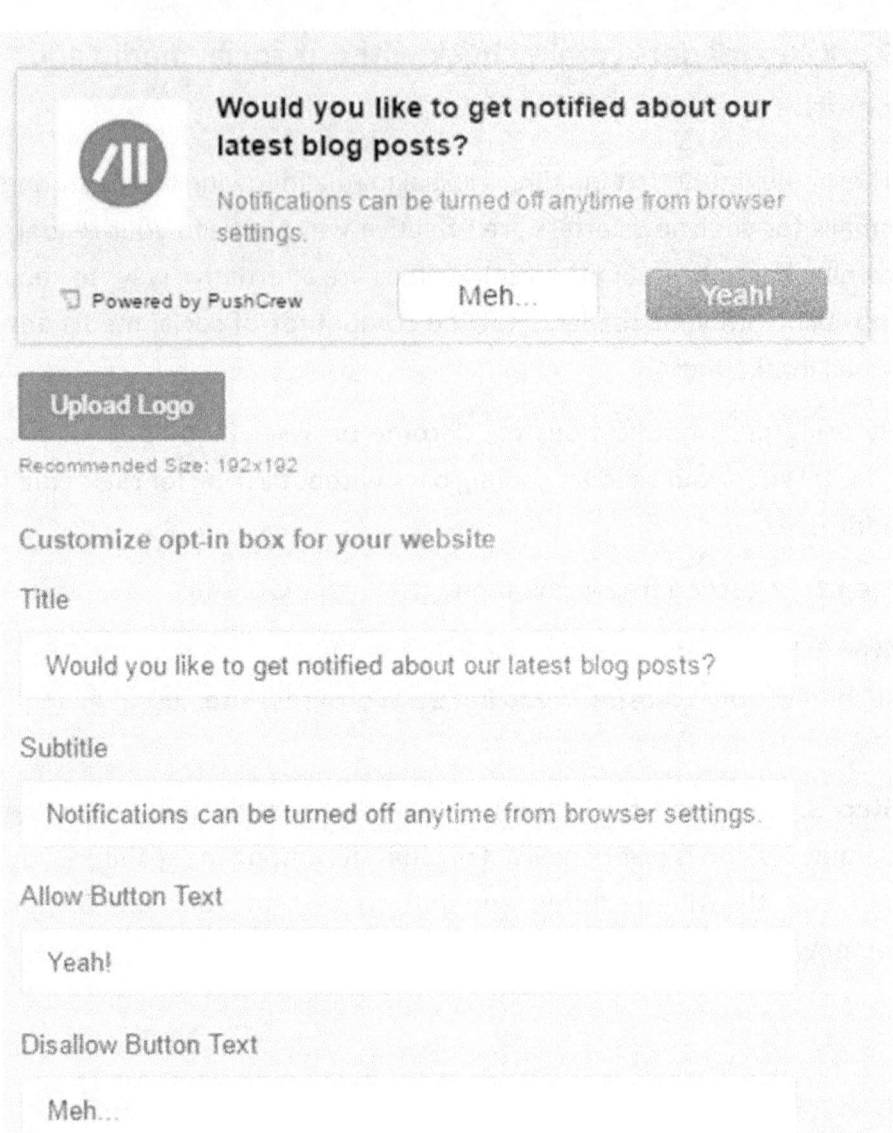

Step 4: All we have to do is set up automatic scheduling notifications for your subscribers. You can use RSS-based notification, which is included in the free package, and your subscribers will be notified 30 minutes after your new post was published. From the left menu, select "RSS-to-Push" and add your website's RSS feed.

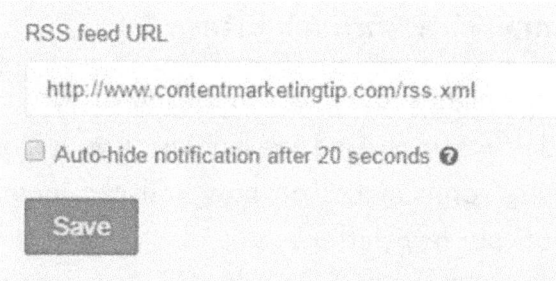

Tools:

PushCrew

GoRoost

PushAssist

Insert headers and footers

Recommended reading:

Before You Send That Push Notification, Read This

Clicks increased by 200%, and subscribers up to four figures – See how Chargebee now pushes its blog-posts

3 Ways to Improve the Performance of Web Push Notifications

92. Boost email click through rates

You can have the highest open rate in the industry, but it isn't worth much if nobody ends up clicking and landing on your blog post. In this tip, I'm showing some tactics on how you can increase the click through rate of your newsletter.

Keep your email short: People are generally busy, so they don't have time to read long emails. If you keep your message short, you can increase the likelihood that your subscribers will actually read and consider your offer. Communicate the benefits of your content clearly.

Add share buttons: According to Econsultancy, including share buttons in your email can generate a 30% higher click-through-rate. Even if your reader isn't interested in your offer, they might know a friend who will find it useful. Eventually, our intention is to get people to our blog who are interested in reading our stuff.

Segment your email list: Lyris Annual Email Optimizer Report revealed that 39% of marketers who segmented their email lists reached higher open rates, lower unsubscribe rates and greater retention. A great way to segment your email list is by asking new subscribers' interest at the registration. Then you can put them into different lists and make sure the content you send is relevant. If you cover different topics in your blog, make sure to do this segmentation.

Add a call to action: Including a clear call to action in your email tells your subscribers what they should do. This CTA could be a simple sentence or an embedded button.

Create a sense of urgency: If you have a free giveaway, an email course or webinar, this tactic could be invaluable. Simply put a limit on your offer, which could be a time or participant limit. It will incentivize your subscribers to take action.

Keep it simple: Don't use fancy HTML templates and big headers since they can distract your readers from your message. Also, the HTML template or other embedded visual elements might not appear correctly in their email client, making their experience even worse. Keep it simple and use only plain text with a link or button attached.

Pro tip: Check the industry benchmarks to see how you're performing.

Recommended reading:

Improve Your Email Click-Through Rate With These 14 Simple Tweaks

11 Sure-Fire Ways to Increase Email Click-Through Rates

Email Marketing Benchmarks

93. Welcome email gold mine

Welcome emails are more powerful than you think. 74.4% of users expect a welcome email when they subscribe and the average open rate for welcome emails is 50% - 86% more effective than email newsletters.

Since welcome emails receive much higher engagement and you shouldn't miss this opportunity to suggest a next step for your new subscribers. Instead of just saying thank you, here are some things you should consider:

- Offer product discount
- Recommend other content to read
- Offer special content to download
- Ask them to forward your email
- Cross sell something
- Encourage subscribers to connect on other channels
- Whitelist your email address

Pro tip: Don't try to ask too many things. Keep your email simple and only ask one thing from your new subscriber.

Tools:

Mailchimp

Getresponse

Recommended reading:

Email marketing statistics 2016

A guide to sending brilliant ecommerce welcome emails

94. Newsletter boost with emojis

Emojis are fun and I'm glad they invaded the world; actually this is my favorite: 🚀.

It's not just a fun way of communication but also a new marketing asset that can be used. Mailjet and Experian conducted research on this topic; they included emojis in their email's subject lines.

The results revealed that different countries and cultures respond to emoji use differently, and not all emojis had the same effect.

Here is what they found:

- 56% of brands experienced an increase in open rates when emojis are included in email subject lines.

- Americans are 43% more likely to open an email if the subject line includes an emoji.

- Brits are 63% more likely to open an email with an emoji accompanying the subject line.

- Across all geographies, the best performing emoji was this with a 31,5% open rate: 😊

If you start using emojis in your email subject line, chances are that you will see an increased open rate for that email. If you're not sure how the emojis will be received by your subscribers, only test them with a very small segment of your email list. If you see an increase in open rates and people didn't get mad seeing an emoji in the subject line, then you should proceed and use emojis for the whole email list.

Tools:

Emojipedia

Mailchimp

Getresponse

Recommended reading:

Infographic: The Performance of Emojis in Email Subject Lines

Thinking about using symbols in your email subject lines?

Emojis and Emails, a Match Made in Heaven (Maybe)

95. Retargeting visitors

Most of your website's first-time visitors leave your site without conversion; only 5-8% of them will convert. Retargeting (or remarketing) can be very effective to recover 95% of leads you thought were lost.

Indeed, users who are retargeted are 70% more likely to convert and retargeting can lead to 147% higher conversion rate. That's pretty good.

In this tip, I'm showing you how to use Facebook retargeting to increase the conversion of your webinars, guides and other giveaways.

Step 1: Before you start doing anything on Facebook, make sure that your Facebook pixel is added to your website's head section. This pixel tracks your audience who have previously visited your website. If your website runs on WordPress, use this plugin to easily edit your header. See the official implementation guide here.

Step 2: After adding this pixel, you should create a custom audience for everyone who visits your website or a specific page on your website. Log in to Business Manager on Facebook and from the menu, select "Audiences".

Step 3: On the left hand side, click "Create audience" and select "Custom

Audience."

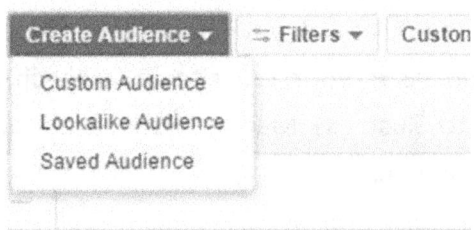

Step 4: From the following window, select "website traffic". Set your audience's details based on their past behavior on your site. I recommend you segment your audience based on what pages they visited on your website.

Website traffic ⓘ	People who visit specific web pages ▼

Include people who visit any web page that meets the following rules.

URL contains ▼	Add URL keywords

In the Last ⓘ	30	days

Audience Name	Enter a name for your audience

Add a description

Step 5: Hit "Create Audience" and we're all set. All you need to do is to wait until your specified page receives a certain amount of traffic. After that, your custom audience will be active and you can start retargeting them with a special offer on Facebook.

Tools:

Insert headers and footers

Recommended reading:

3 Marvelous Behavioral Retargeting Hacks For Power Marketers

Retargeting: The 10 Stats you Probably Didnt Know

8 Best Practices for Retargeting on Facebook

96. Improve subscriber list quality

There are many ways you can achieve higher open and click through rates for your newsletter. I already mentioned a few and I'm sure you can find several other useful tactics online.

Even if your emails are fully optimized with battle tested subject lines and calls to action, it's possible that you still didn't see significant improvement in email engagement. In this case, the problem is probably not the quality of your email, but the quality of your subscribers. It's called the graymail problem.

Graymail is email your visitors opted in to receive, but they don't really want it anymore.

Although it's not considered spam, sending graymail is problematic because it can hurt the deliverability of your email overall. Low engagement rate could be an indicator for email clients to put your email to the junk folder. This is what Hubspot's marketing blog was facing.

They decided to take action and unsubscribed every subscriber who hit a certain threshold of engagement (everyone who hadn't clicked on an email in the last six months). They actually removed 45% of their subscribers. Boom.

Sounds really weird, but put it this way. The number of your subscribers is a big vanity metric. You could have 10,000 subscribers with 100 people engaging with your emails or 5,000 subscribers with 100 engaging. The bottom line is the same.

By eliminating inactive subscribers, the quality of your email list will improve, which leads to higher open rates, and email clients won't consider your emails as spam so the deliverability remains good.

If you want to do the same for your subscriber list, check out these guides for Mailchimp and Getresponse.

Recommended reading:

Never Heard of 'Graymail'? Here's What You Need to Know

Why We Unsubscribed 250K People From HubSpot's Marketing Blog & Started Sending Less Email

Part 10: Other Tips

97. Blog post commenting

You can easily capitalize on the traffic of the most popular blog posts in your niche. All you have to do is to leave a comment on these posts. But before you start copy-pasting the same comment with your link, it's super important to read the whole article and add a meaningful comment. You have to say something that is related to that article and adds value to the conversation. Otherwise, it's just a nicely wrapped creepy spam and your comment won't be allowed. Don't even try to leave a comment like this: "Great article; check out this: <Random link>.

Step 1: Do a Google search for the topic keywords you have covered in your post. Make it as narrow as possible for better targeting and relevance.

Step 2: Do a similar search on Buzzsumo to find the most shared articles in that topic.

Step 3: Create a list of articles and keep the ones where commenting is allowed.

Step 4: Prioritize this list and focus only on the top-ranking and most shared articles.

Step 5: Leave a comment if it's applicable.

Pro tip: Get notified of new posts by tracking newly published articles in your niche. Just add focus keywords that describe your topic to Google Alerts or Mention. Every time a new post is published containing your keyword, you will be notified.

Tools:

Buzzsumo

Google Alerts

Mention

Recommended reading:

How To Generate Insane Volumes Of Traffic Through Blog Commenting

How To Craft A Blog Comment That Will Generate Traffic And Get You Noticed

How to Blog Comment Your Way to Consistent Traffic Growth

How to Increase Your Traffic and SEO by Commenting

98. Write a teaser on Medium.com

Medium.com is a popular blogging platform. It has a plain, simple design and a super easy setup process so you don't really have to worry about the technical details. You can focus on creating awesome content. When you register at Medium.com with your Twitter account, everyone who is your follower on Twitter and is also registered on Medium.com will be your follower on Medium as well, so you don't have to build a follower base from scratch. You can use this platform to drive traffic to your blog. *(Hint - if you don't have many followers, then check out tip 14 to learn how to get 1000 followers within a week).*

Step 1: Register at Medium.com with your Twitter profile.

Step 2: Once your post is published on your blog, write a 300-400 word teaser on Medium.com.

Step 3: Make sure that you include links in the body of your post and to the bottom of the Medium post so your readers can easily visit your website and read the original post. You can place a short call to action like this: "Click here to keep reading and to get some actionable tips!"

Don't just copy and paste text from your blog post. Instead, create an original post so you can avoid a duplicate content penalty from Google.

Tools:

Medium

Recommended reading:

The Marketer's Guide To Medium

How to Use Medium: The Complete Guide to Medium for Marketers

How to Get More Traffic from Every Post by Republishing on Medium

99. Slow mo is no go

Amazon found out that 100ms of latency cost them 1% in sales. You can imagine what this means for a huge site like Amazon.

According to CrazyEgg, a 1-second delay in a page load time yields 11% fewer page views, a 16% decrease in customer satisfaction and a 7% loss in conversion.

Slow website loading time not only decreases conversion, but is also a factor that matters when your site is ranked by Google.

Step 1: Is your website in slow mo? Check its speed with Google's free tool. It not only scores your website but also suggests changes to improve its performance. If it's considered slow, it's time to dig deeper.

Step 2: Enter your URL to this website speed tester to show exactly how long it takes for your website to load.

Step 3: In most cases, you need developer help to resolve the highlighted issues. What you can do is a tool audit and consider replacing or eliminating tools that load when your website is triggered.

Tools:

Google's Speed Tester

Website Speed Test

Recommended reading:

10 Ways to Speed Up Your Website – and Improve Conversion by 7%

How to Speed up Website (WordPress) without Changing Web Host

How to Improve Your Page Load Speed by 70.39% in 45 Minutes

100. Email signature

If you send out a lot of emails, you might want to try this tip. You won't get tons of traffic from this tactic, but it takes just a few minutes to set everything up. So why not give it a try? We're creating an email signature for you that points back to your blog or your latest blog post.

Step 1: You need to actually write your email signature in your email client. In Gmail, go to settings and select "General" from the menu. Scroll down until you see the "Signature" label.

Step 2: In the text field, write your name and you can even add your title as well. Make sure you also mention either your blog or your latest blog post. You can do it by simply asking questions in your signature; for example: Do you want to get more traffic? Check out my tips here.

Step 3: Select the link you would like to include in your signature and add UTM parameters to it by using this free tool so we can track if someone visits your blog by clicking on your signature.

Tools:

New Old Stamp

Wise Stamp

UTM Link Generator

Recommended reading:

Intro to UTM Parameters and Best Practices

How To Write A Damn Good Email Signature

Signature examples

12 Clever Ways to Use Your Email Signature to Support Your Marketing Campaigns

Bonus Resources

You can get instant access to 5 additional tips, downloadable worksheets, checklists, a list of resources and links mentioned in this book.

I highly recommend you unlock this bonus package to get the most out of this book.

CONTENTMARKETINGTIP.COM/RESOURCES

Please share this book with others

Did you enjoy the book? It would be awesome if you could share it with your friends on social media. Just click the links below to share. It really takes just two clicks.

Twitter - Facebook - LinkedIn - Google Plus

Books you need to read

Mom test: How to talk to customers & learn if your business is a good idea when everyone is lying to you.

The Entrepreneur's Guide to Customer Development: A cheat sheet to The Four Steps to the Epiphany

Ask: The counter-intuitive online formula to discover exactly what your customers want to buy

Everybody Writes: Your Go-To Guide to Creating Ridiculously Good Content

Content Inc.: How Entrepreneurs Use Content to Build Massive Audiences and Create Radically Successful Businesses

Contagious: Why Things Catch On

Made to Stick: Why Some Ideas Survive and Others Die

Purple Cow, New Edition: Transform Your Business by Being Remarkable

Launch: An Internet Millionaire's Secret Formula to Sell Almost Anything Online

About the author

Tamas Torok is a self-taught online marketer, focusing on content marketing. He learned marketing on the go, quite often the hard way. Apart from creating paper planes, he mostly works with startups and other companies to build and improve their online marketing.

He simply can't stop learning and experimenting with new things. He is determined to create his own smartphone game so he started learning to code.

He has lived in Sweden and in England. Now, he's living in Hungary.

Feel free to connect him on Twitter and LinkedIn or just drop him a mail: tamas@contentmarketingtip.com

Thank you

I was lucky to have my own tribe, a group of awesome content marketers who were always with me on the rough road of writing. Some of them helped me to get started, others provided insanely detailed feedback on my ideas and there were some who always had a few kind words that kept me going on melancholic rainy days. Thank you guys for being here and for your incredible support. I couldn't make it without you.

Special thanks to:

Adam J. Fleischer

Adam Maidment

Adelle Kehoe

Alexandra Gulkin

Amanda McGrath

Amy Jordan

Andrew Dennis

Annem Hobson

Annie Qadeer

Antonio Lamborizio

Arthur Luke

Bobby Stemper

Brandon Fong

Brian Lang

Charlotte Poynton

Chris Bibey

Christopher

Benitez

Craig Kilgore

Damian McNamara

Dan Goss

Daniel Taibleson

Danielle Papsis

David Hartshorne

David Hoos

Dayana Stockdale

Duke Stewart

Elif Ozgecan Celik

Eric Novakovics

Erin Palmer

Ettie Holland

Gian Luca

Greg Gascon

Heta Dave

HilLesha O'Nan

Holly Pels

Jacob Rouser

James Larson

Jarrett Kruse

Jennifer Le Roux

Jennifer Morilla

Jeri Denniston

Jim Gallant

Joanne Dewberry

Jordan Lore

Jose Angelo Gallegos

Joseph Rauch

Julie Scheurer

Karla Socci Somers

Kasia Manolas

Kathleen de Lara

Kevin Kelly

Kristen Marrs

Laura Pearson-Smith

Lionel Valdellon

Lisa Diesel

Lisa Ivaldi

Louise Kilburn

Loz James

Luca Rosi

Lucy Wray

Marius Kiniulis

Mark Thomas

Mathew Passy

Matt Banner

Matthew Goldman

May Chau

Mia Major

Michael Becker

Michael Karp

Michael Weisbaum

Michelle Luo

Milly Youngman

Monika Ribeiro

Morgan J. Staub

Pat Ahern

Pat E. Layton

Patricia Browne

Philip Hoey

Pierre Roustan

Rachel Andrea

Ray White

Raymond Manley

Rhian Wilkinson

Ross Francis Duncan

Ryan Robinson

Sarah Poloske-James

Saskia van Nieuwenhuizen

Shad Connelly

Sophorn Chhay

Stacy Solomon

Stefanie Mauro

Steve McOrmond

Tanya Adams

Taylor Freitas

Tierney Young

Tom Rapsas

Valentina Giannella

Vinny La Barbera

Wensy Duong

Will Robins

Thanks for the support to:

AJ Ogaard

Aki Merced

Alexandra Bohigian

Alexandra Coxon

Alicia Thomas

Amada Dorta

Amanda Stewart

Amanda Webb

Anderson Conte

Andrew Littlefield

Angelica Hay

Anne Felicitas

Arsene Lavaux

Autumn Sullivan

Barbara McLullich

Barry Katzmann

Brandon Darnton

Brett Dalton

Cache Walker

Cara Hogan

Catherine Brown

Cecilia Haynes

Dallan Isom

Dennis Williams

Derek J. Hernandez

Ellie Hubble

Emily Beeson

Emily Rose

Emma Humphrey

Ezekiel Rudick

Gabrielle Balestrier

Hailey Brown

Henning Okholm

Henry Adaso

Henry McIntosh

Jackie James

Jane Haynie

Jennifer Boidy

Jennifer Parkerson

Jennifer Smith

Jesse Davis

Jessica Cates

Jon Lewis

Jonathan Cohn

Kyle Cassidy

Lucas Miller

Lucy Hitz

Mai Copso

Maria Onzain

Marta Romeu Pérez

Mathieu Rainville

Michael Bergen

Ngan Ton

Nicholas Stutzman

Nikki McCaig

Nneya Richards

Ohad Flinker

Philippa Brangam

Rachel Wish

Rand Owens

Rena Iglehart

Rilee Chastain

Robert Medak

Rodney C. Jones

Samantha Feller

Scott Malmberg

Siobhan Baranian

Terrence Johnson

Tyler Munn

Veronika Janeckova

William Ellis

William McNish

www.ingramcontent.com/pod-product-compliance
Lightning Source LLC
Chambersburg PA
CBHW061436180526
45170CB00004B/1428